CREATING AN INCLUSIVE SCHOOL

RICHARD A. VILLA
AND
JACQUELINE S. THOUSAND,
EDITORS

Kris Beall

Association for Supervision
and Curriculum Development
Alexandria, Virginia

ASCD

Association for Supervision and Curriculum Development
1250 N. Pitt Street • Alexandria, VA 22314
Telephone: (703) 549-9110 • Fax: (703) 549-3891

Printed in the United States of America.

Gene R. Carter, *Executive Director*
Michelle Terry, *Assistant Executive Director, Program Development*
Ronald S. Brandt, *Assistant Executive Director*
Nancy Modrak, *Managing Editor, ASCD Books*
Carolyn R. Pool, *Associate Editor*

Stephanie Justen, *Assistant Editor*
Gary Bloom, *Manager, Design and Production Services*
Karen Monaco, *Senior Graphic Designer*
Tracey A. Smith, *Print Production Coordinator*
Valerie Sprague, *Desktop Publisher*

ASCD Stock No. 195210   Price $15.95   cp 11/95

Library of Congress Cataloging-in-Publication Data
Creating an inclusive school / Richard A. Villa and Jacqueline S.
    Thousand, editors.
        p. cm.
    "ASCD Stock No. 195210"—T.p. verso.
    Includes bibliographical references.
    ISBN 0-87120-251-4 (pbk.)
    1. Handicapped children—Education—United States.
    2. Mainstreaming in education—United States. 3. School management
    and organization—United States. I. Villa, Richard A., 1952-
    II. Thousand, Jacqueline S., 1950-
    LC4031.C74 1995
    371.9'046—dc20   95-32532
                                                                    CIP

10   9   8   7   6   5   4   3   2   1

Creating an Inclusive School

Foreword

Discussions on inclusion provoke strong and often differing opinions among educators. These differences are evident in the December 1994/January 1995 issue of *Educational Leadership*, "The Inclusive School." For example, Albert Shanker, President of the American Federation of Teachers, questions the concept in his article, "Full Inclusion Is Neither Free Nor Appropriate." But several educators from the Gwinnett County, Georgia, Public Schools offer a different perspective in their article, "How Inclusion Built a Community of Learners."

Contributors to *Creating an Inclusive School* express strong support for inclusive educational practices. In the opening chapter, the authors note that "institutions teach by example what a country, state, or community values—inclusion or segregation and exclusion."

The authors trace the legal background to inclusive education. They state: "Although the terms *inclusion* or *inclusive education* cannot be located in the law, the provision for *least restrictive environment* provided the legal impetus for inclusive education." What is inclusion or inclusive education? The authors note that it is an attitude or belief system, not an action or set of actions. Inclusion is "a way of life, a way of living together, based on a belief that each individual is valued and does belong." An inclusive school will be one in which all students feel included. The editors of this book, Richard Villa and Jacqueline Thousand, present a constellation of rationales for inclusion, including our changing assumptions of how children learn, demographic changes, shifts in funding, and demonstrations of effective programs. They ask: "Which rationale is most compelling for you?"

Throughout this book, you will discover some moving and compelling "voices of inclusion." These are stories by teachers and parents of students participating in inclusive classrooms, as well as a reflection by an adult with a disability—and his spouse. Regardless of your feelings about inclusion, I promise you will be affected by one of the "voices" of inclusion: "Everything About Bob Was Cool, Including the Cookies."

Educational leaders who wish to provide inclusive educational experiences for students with disabilities will benefit from the authors' experience in managing change in education. After identifying the factors that have made school organizations resistant to change, the authors examine the variables that can contribute to successful organizational change—and to more inclusionary programs. The authors of this book identify promising practices and extensive resources for classroom teachers wishing to implement some inclusion initiatives—and curriculum adaptations—to meet the needs of a diverse student population.

Disagreements continue among parents, educators, and community members in regard to inclusive education. In one chapter, seven authors collaborated to answer 16 of the most commonly asked questions about inclusion. This familiar question is an example: "Are inclusion advocates primarily concerned with socialization? Are academics being satisfied?" Although your individual perspective will greatly influence your responses to the questions, the comments of the individuals who collaborated on the responses will stimulate your thinking and provide you with a broader perspective on the issue.

This book is a valuable addition to the literature on inclusion. Although the authors state that inclusion is still an elusive and confusing term, I am certain this book will bring focus and clarity to the debate.

CHARLES E. PATTERSON
1995–96 ASCD President

1

What Is an Inclusive School?

Mary A. Falvey, Christine C. Givner, and Christina Kimm

> There is only one child in the world and that child's name is
> ALL children.
>
> —Carl Sandburg

An Inclusive Classroom in Action

It is Monday morning, the third week in October, and students are arriving at school by foot, bicycle, wheelchair, school bus, public bus, and family vehicles. Younghee, Anthony, Jelani, and Nathan are talking together on the grass in front of the school when José, being pushed in his wheelchair by his step-sister Maria, goes by. Immediately, all four of the students stop what they are doing to ask José if he is going to the Halloween carnival planned for the following Saturday. José replies with a big smile and nod, which, for those who know him, translates to "Yes, definitely."

They were *all* going—now they just needed to determine what, if any, costumes they would wear. (When you are in 5th grade, the "rules" are not firm about whether it would be inappropriate to wear a costume.) Since these students are all assigned to the same classroom (except for José's sister), Maria motions to someone in the group to grab José's wheelchair handles. Jelani does, and they all proceed to their classroom.

They greet their teacher, Ms. Rosenberg, as they enter the classroom, and hang up their backpacks. Everyone spends a few minutes socializing and enjoying a little free time. Ms. Rosenberg rings a bell to signal the students to get ready for class. They put away their comic books, baseball cards, and other belongings and gather in the front of the room. Ms. Rosenberg greets them and reviews the day's schedule, which includes a visitor. She explains the visitor's purpose and approximate time of arrival. The students discuss the schedule and other business during this daily class meeting.

The visitor is Ms. Olson, a physical therapist. José used to go somewhere else with Ms. Olson during physical education (P.E.) class, but last week the class learned that from now on he would be having P.E. with everyone else. Since José would participate in P.E. for the first time today, Ms. Olson meets with the class to discuss his participation and what others might do to help with his inclusion in P.E. She explains what a physical therapist does and seeks questions from the class.

Younghee asks if anyone can push José's wheelchair during P.E. and if there were any special ways to push his wheelchair during kickball. (José has been a part of the class for four months, but Younghee hadn't yet interacted very much with him.) Ms. Olson asks José what he thought about being pushed by anybody as long as they asked him first.

José, using his communication device, replies, "Okay."

Ms. Olson adds, "Try going backwards when you go down a slope, especially when coming from the auditorium, because it is quite steep." Ms. Olson then asks the students if they have any ideas for helping José "kick" the ball since he cannot move his leg or foot.

One student suggests a "pinch" kicker while José is pushed around the bases; another student suggests that José use a baseball bat attached to his wheelchair while someone pushes him.

Ms. Olson shows the students how José, with a partner, can participate in a stretching activity. She asks for a volunteer for a demonstration. Mary volunteers, and is instructed to hold José's hands to stretch, which makes José giggle. Mary immediately releases his hands, thinking she is hurting him. Ms. Olson assures her that she did not hurt him and that he is just being silly. José nods his head and smiles in agreement. Mary and José demonstrate several stretching activities they can do together.

Ms. Olson tells the class that for awhile she will come twice a week during P.E. and that everyone should ask her any questions that come to mind. She thanks the students for their attention and all their great ideas.

After Ms. Olson leaves, the students participate in small-group discussions about the projects in which they are working that relate to the contributions of people who died for a cause, country, or world peace. This activity uses an integrated approach to the curriculum where language arts, social studies, art, and social skills are the integrated goals.

José's group includes Anthony, Jelani, Nathan, and Younghee. Anthony and José have typed their description into a computer. Anthony is interested in computers, so he is happy to have the opportunity to work with José on his computer. José is learning to use the computer with an adaptive switch that activates and controls the cursor. Jelani has written and recorded a song representing his perspective. Younghee has cut out magazines to create a collage of her thoughts with a peer who wrote the description that Younghee dictated. Nathan has painted a series of pictures depicting what the world would look like filled with peace. They had to do lots of research and work for this group project, and all the students in the group wanted to do their best job.

One of the other groups has decided to invite some parents to speak. Chung's father is going to talk about his experiences living in Vietnam during the Vietnam War. Ms. Rosenberg needs to ask for an interpreter for Chung's father, since he speaks Vietnamese fluently but English only a little. Michael's mother will talk about an African American soldier, Nathan's older brother, who died during the "Desert Storm" operation. Finally, Ms. Rosenberg's class decides to have an open house at the end of the semester to display what they have learned.

❧   ❧   ❧

Of the 32 fourth and fifth graders in Ms. Rosenberg's class, 16 speak Spanish fluently and have limited abilities to understand and speak English. Two students speak and understand Korean fluently with only a little English. These students' needs present an opportunity for Ms.

Rosenberg to demonstrate her skills at teaching second-language acquisition. Specifically, she uses English as a Second Language (ESL) strategies such as total physical response, sheltered English strategies, and
structuring of interactive and "hands-on" activities (Genesee 1987;
Krashen 1982; Richard-Amato and Snow 1992).

The heterogeneity of the students in this class reflects the growing
diversity in most classrooms throughout the United States. Many of
these children were previously labeled and forced into categories that
limited their exposure to one another, essential curriculum, and the use
of a variety of instructional procedures and personnel. This is a real
classroom—and these are real children, all eager and struggling to learn
and be the most they can be. In the past, Jelani and three or four other
students would have been labeled "gifted" and removed and placed in
a gifted and talented program; José, Younghee, and one or two other
students would have been classified as disabled and placed in a segregated special education program; and the students speaking languages
other than English would have been placed in separate bilingual programs where they would have limited exposure to English-speaking
children in their school.

Some people argue that the social justice occurring in this scenario—
inclusive education—is not the responsibility of schools. However, if
not the schools, then whose responsibility is it? It is our systems and
institutions that teach by example what a country, state, or community
values—inclusion, or segregation and exclusion. Inclusive education
demands that a country's system supporting and educating students
create and provide whatever is necessary to ensure that all students
have access to meaningful learning. It does not require students to
possess any particular set of skills or abilities (Falvey 1995).

Legal Definition of Inclusive Education

The legal mandate driving inclusive education in the United States
is Public Law 94-142 (now the Individuals with Disabilities Education
Act, IDEA). Although the terms *inclusion* or *inclusive education* cannot
be located in this law, the definition of least restrictive environment
(LRE) is contained in the law and has provided the initial legal impetus
for creating inclusive education. The law states that:

to the maximum extent appropriate, handicapped children, including those children in public and private institutions or other care facilities, are educated with children who are not handicapped, and that special classes, separate schooling, or other removal of handicapped children from the regular educational environment occurs only when the nature or severity of the handicap is such that education in regular classes with the use of supplementary aids and services cannot be achieved satisfactorily (P.L. 94-142, Section 1412 [5] [B]).

The critical term used in the law is "with the use of supplementary aids and services." In 1975, when P.L. 94-142 was passed, the professional education literature was void of any information or strategies for using supplementary aids and services to effectively include students with disabilities. However, since that time, the use of supplementary aids and services to effectively include all students has been frequently identified and described in the literature (e.g., Falvey 1995; Stainback and Stainback 1992; Thousand, Villa, and Nevin 1994). As a result, the LRE mandate has been a leading force in the design and implementation of inclusive education.

The LRE principle, however, is not without its critics. Steven Taylor, in his critical analysis based on previous critical analyses, describes the following seven conceptual and philosophical flaws and pitfalls of LRE:

1. The LRE principle legitimates settings that are restrictive.

2. The LRE equates intensity of services with the degree of amount of integration.

3. The LRE principle is based upon a "readiness model."

4. The LRE principle promotes professionals decision making over others.

5. The LRE principle sanctions infringements on people's rights.

6. The LRE principle implies that people should move as they develop and change.

7. The LRE principle focuses on physical settings rather than on services and supports people need to be successfully included in community settings (Taylor 1988).

Despite the criticism of Taylor and others, the LRE mandate resulted in the development of "mainstreaming" or "integration." These terms, also not contained in the law, reflect initial attempts at questioning and rejecting the segregation and isolation of people with disabilities. Mainstreaming and integration of students with disabilities in general education settings often resulted in students' part-time enrollment in general education classes. In addition, mainstreaming often required that students with disabilities achieve a predetermined criteria level before they could participate in general education, otherwise known as a "readiness model."

We know from the literature (McIntosh, Vaughn, Schumm, Haager, and Lee 1993; Zigmond and Baker 1990) and from our experience that mainstreaming and integration failed enormous numbers of students; however, this failure has not been because the students were not ready. Decisions about whether to mainstream students often were arbitrary and capricious; and students were provided with insufficient or ineffective supports when they entered general education classrooms. Although well meaning, mainstreaming and integration as an educational program model became a disaster in need of a major overhaul.

In 1986, the U.S. Department of Education issued the "regular education initiative," which was an attempt to encourage special educators to develop a partnership to work closely with general educators to effectively educate students with disabilities (Will 1986). New strategies were called for to more effectively educate these students in general education classrooms. As a result, schools and school districts began experimenting with a variety of strategies for educating these students, which specifically led to the development of inclusive education.

However, just as in race relations, interventions by the federal courts have been necessary to help define inclusive education. For example, in *Sacramento Unified School District v. Holland* (1994), the U.S. Supreme Court refused to consider changing the lower federal court decision that required the school district to create the supports necessary to include Rachel, a student with developmental disabilities in general education classes.

Pragmatic Definition of Inclusive Education

So what is inclusion or inclusive education? First, it is an attitude—a value and belief system—not an action or set of actions. Once adopted by a school or school district, it should drive all decisions and actions by those who have adopted it. The word *include* implies being a part of something, being embraced into the whole. *Exclude*, the antonym of *include*, means to keep out, to bar, or to expel. These definitions begin to frame the growing movement of building inclusive schools. The very meaning of the terms *inclusion* and *exclusion* helps us to understand inclusive education.

What does it feel like to be included and excluded? Thousands of children, adolescents, and adults have been asked by the authors of this chapter and the editors of this text to identify an event in their lives in which they felt included, and one in which they felt excluded, as well as to identify how they felt during and following these two experiences. Figure 1.1 provides a sampling of the feelings people have shared when they felt included and when they felt excluded.

The results of this exercise provide a good introduction to this book, which focuses on strategies for ensuring that schools embrace and

FIGURE 1.1 Responses to the Question, "How did it feel when you were . . ."	
Excluded?	**Included?**
• angry	• proud
• resentful	• secure
• hurt	• special
• frustrated	• comfortable
• lonely	• recognized
• different	• confident
• confused	• happy
• isolated	• excited
• inferior	• trusted
• worthless	• cared about
• invisible	• liked
• substandard	• accepted
• unwanted	• appreciated
• untrusted	• reinforced
• unaccepted	• loved
• closed	• grateful
• ashamed	• normal
	• open
	• positive
	• nurtured
	• important
	• responsible
	• grown up

educate all students, not just select ones that fit some preconceived notion of "educable." The emotions listed in the figure make the powerful point that no one wants to be excluded. Inclusive education is about embracing all, making a commitment to do whatever it takes to provide each student in the community—and each citizen in a democracy—an inalienable right to belong, not to be excluded. Inclusion assumes that living and learning together is a better way that benefits everyone, not just children who are labeled as having a difference (e.g., gifted, non-English proficient, or disability).

Pearpoint and Forest (1992) describe the important underlying values of an inclusive school as the ABCs (Acceptance, Belonging, and Community) and the three Rs (Reading, Writing, and Relationships). An inclusive school values interdependence as well as independence. It values its students, staff, faculty, and parents as a community of learners. An inclusive school views each child as gifted. An inclusive school cherishes and honors all kinds of diversity as an opportunity for learning about what makes us human. Inclusion focuses on how to support the special gifts and needs of each and every student in the school community to feel welcomed and secure and to become successful. Another assumption underlying inclusive schooling is that good teaching is good teaching, that each child can learn, given the appropriate environment, encouragement, and meaningful activities. Inclusive schools base curriculum and daily learning activities on everything known about good teaching and learning.

Implications of Inclusive Education

Inclusion is the opposite of segregation and isolation. Segregated, specialized education creates a permanent underclass of students, with a strong message to these students that they do not "cut the mustard," and that they do not fit or belong. Segregation assumes that the right to belong is earned rather than an unconditional human right. Norman Kunc (1992) speaks of the casualties of exclusion or "conditional acceptance." He describes many of the current problems facing children and youth at risk (e.g., gangs, suicide, and dropping out) as being casualties of an inflexible, insensitive system of education that systematically (perhaps unintentionally) destroys the self-esteem and self-worth of students who do not "fit the mold." In a seminal work that describes the plight of our youth at risk, from a Native American perspective,

Brendtro, Brokenleg, and Van Bockern (1990) describe *belonging* as one of the four central values that create a child's "Circle of Courage." The authors state that the right to "belong is not only a cultural belonging of Native people, but a cultural birthright for all the world's children" (p. 36). Given the increasing numbers of students labeled "at risk," and the centrality of the need to belong, schools must provide a vehicle for reclaiming youth labeled "at risk," disabled, homeless, gay or lesbian, and so forth.

The growing diversity of our student population is a topic of great debate and concern. Diversity differences may include language, culture, religion, gender, disability, sexual preference, socioeconomic status, geographic setting, and more. Diversity often is spoken about as if it were a plight rather than a wonderful opportunity for learning, that is, learning about the rich variety of each others' lives and also learning about what it is to be human—to be included, to be valued and respected for just who we are in a naturally diverse world.

Inclusive Education and School Restructuring

The call for restructuring of American education to establish meaningful educational standards (i.e., student outcomes) and to hold schools accountable for accomplishing these outcomes with each and every student, requires great human commitment and effort, individually and collectively. This commitment requires that we believe that each child can learn and succeed, that diversity enriches us all, that students at risk for failure can overcome that risk through involvement in a thoughtful and caring community of learners, that each child has unique contributions to offer to the community of learners, that each child has strengths and needs, and that effective learning results from the collaborative efforts of us all to ensure the success of each student.

Systems-change initiatives in special education are paralleling similar efforts in general education, often referred to as school restructuring. Educators and researchers are raising fundamental questions regarding the most effective strategies for teaching all students; and many people are designing and implementing numerous innovative and highly effective strategies. Chapters 4–6 describe the following school restructuring efforts in greater detail:

• Teachers are using heterogeneous and cooperative group arrangements of students because these strategies are more effective for learning (Oakes 1985; Sapon-Shevin 1994).

• As a result of having high expectations for all students (Levin 1992), many educators are providing students with individualized approaches to curriculum, assessment (e.g., nonbiased assessment procedures, multiple approaches to intelligence) (Armstrong 1987), and instruction.

• Staff, students, parents, and the community are collaborating with one another in the design and delivery of effective education for all students (Villa and Thousand 1992; Thousand, Villa, and Nevin 1994).

• Teachers and other professionals are giving students the opportunity to learn to think and be creative, and not just repeat information learned (Costa 1991).

• School staff are facilitating students' social skills as they interact, relate to one another, and develop relationships and friendships (Noddings 1992).

As the characteristics of the school restructuring movement take hold in more and more schools, inclusion of students with disability labels does not become a separate and distinct action; instead, it occurs simultaneously and naturally. The characteristics of both the school restructuring movement and building of inclusive schools are the same: all students experiencing quality education that meets their own educational needs in the context of political and social justice.

We have offered a variety of perspectives on a definition of inclusive schools. We do not subscribe to any one definition. We believe, however, that we *must* create, cherish, and nurture schools that include and effectively educate all of their students.

Inclusion is not just for students with disabilities, but rather for all the students, educators, parents, and community members. Experience tells us that as communities and schools embrace the true meaning of inclusion, they will be better equipped to learn about and acquire strategies to change a segregated special education system to an inclusive service delivery system, with meaningful, child-centered learning. In the process, a society and world intolerant and fearful of difference may change to one that embraces and celebrates its natural diversity. As York (1994) states, inclusion involves students' "attendance in the same schools as siblings and neighbors, membership in general education classrooms with chronological age appropriate classmates, having individualized and relevant learning objectives, and being provided with the support necessary to learn (e.g., special education and related services)" (p. 3).

Even after it is operationally defined, inclusion is still an elusive term. Part of the confusion arises from the varying assumptions that people associate with inclusive education—for example, that it is a "program" or that it is a research-devised strategy. The underlying assumption, however, is that inclusion is a way of life, a way of living together, based on a belief that each individual is valued and does belong.

References

Armstrong, T. (1987). *In Their Own Way.* Los Angeles: Jeremy P. Tarcher, Inc.

Baker, J., and N. Zigmond. (1990). "Are Regular Education Classes Equipped to Accommodate Students with Learning Disabilities?" *Exceptional Children* 56: 515–526.

Brendtro, L. K., M. Brokenleg, and S. Van Bockern. (1990). *Reclaiming Youth at Risk: Our Hope for the Future.* Bloomington, Ind.: National Educational Service.

Costa, A. L. (1991). *Developing Minds,* Vol. 1. Alexandria, Va.: Association for Supervision and Curriculum Development.

Falvey, M. (1995). *Inclusive and Heterogeneous Schooling: Assessment, Curriculum, and Instruction.* Baltimore: Paul H. Brookes.

Genesee, F. (1987). *Learning Through Two Languages.* New York: Harper and Row.

Krashen, S. (1982). *Principles and Practices in Second Language Acquisition.* Oxford, England: Pergamon Press.

Kunc, M. (1992). "The Need to Belong: Rediscovering Maslow's Hierarchy of Needs." In *Restructuring for Caring and Effective Education: An Administrative Guide to Creating Heterogeneous Schools* (pp. 25–40), edited by R.A. Villa, J.S. Thousand, W. Stainback, and S. Stainback. Baltimore: Paul H. Brookes.

Levin, H. (1992). *Accelerated Schools for At-risk Students.* New Bruinswick, N.J.: Center for Policy Research in Education, Rutgers University.

McIntosh, R. S. Vaughn, J.S. Schumm, D. Haager, and O. Lee. (1993). "Observations of Students with Learning Disabilities in General Education Classrooms." *Exceptional Children* 60, 3: 249–261.

Noddings, N. (1992). *The Challenge to Care in Schools: An Alternative Approach to Education*. New York: Teachers College Press.

Oakes, J. (1985). *Keeping Track: How Schools Structure Inequality*. New Haven: Yale University Press.

Pearpoint, J., and M. Forest. (1992). "Foreword." In *Curriculum Considerations in Inclusive Classrooms: Facilitating Learning for All Students* (pp. xv–xviii), edited by S. Stainback and W. Stainback. Baltimore: Paul H. Brookes.

Richard-Amato, P.A., and M.A. Snow. (1992). "Strategies for Content-Area Teachers." In *Readings for Content-Area Teachers*. (pp. 145–163), edited by P.A. Richard-Amato and M.A. Snow. New York: Longman.

Sacramento City Unified School District v. Rachel Holland, No. 92-15608 (9th Cir. 1994).

Sapon-Shevin, M. (1994). *Playing Favorites: Gifted Education and the Disruption of Community*. New York: State University of New York Press.

Stainback, S., and W. Stainback, eds. (1992). *Curriculum Considerations in Inclusive Classrooms: Facilitating Learning for All Students*. Baltimore: Paul H. Brookes.

Taylor, S.J. (1988). "Caught in the Continuum: A Critical Analysis of the Principle of Least Restrictive Environment." *Journal of the Association for Persons with Severe Handicaps* 13, 1: 41–53.

Thousand, J.S., R.A. Villa, and A.I. Nevin, eds. (1994). *Creativity and Collaborative Learning: A Practical Guide to Empowering Students and Teachers*. Baltimore: Paul H. Brookes.

Villa, R.A., and J.S. Thousand. (1992). "Restructuring Public Schools Systems: Strategies for Organizational Change and Progress." In *Restructuring for Caring and Effective Education: An Administrative Guide to Creating Heterogeneous Schools* (pp. 109–140), edited by R.A. Villa, J.S. Thousand, W. Stainback, and S. Stainback. Baltimore: Paul H. Brookes.

Will, M. (1986). "Educating Children with Learning Problems: A Shared Responsibility." *Exceptional Children* 52: 411–415.

York, J. (Spring/Summer 1994). *What's Working*. Minneapolis: Institute on Community Integration, University of Minnesota.

Voice of Inclusion: I'm Just a "Regular Parent"

Jeff Tate

Our future depends on not acting out of fear, but allowing for diversity.
—Norman Kunc

My son is seven years old. He attends a small country school in central Texas. He is in a "regular" 1st grade classroom. This year before his Christmas break, Joey learned that kids who are "different" don't belong in his classroom. This year, my oldest son Joey has learned to read, to write, and to fear diversity.

There was a little boy in Joey's class who couldn't read like the other children. He couldn't keep up with how everyone else was learning. This little boy learned things differently from the other children in Joey's class. Because the boy's teacher had no training in how to create an individualized reading program, the boy cried. He couldn't keep up. There was not a place for him. He was removed from Joey's class and placed in a special segregated class. One day he was there—and another day, because he learned differently, he was removed.

A brutal tragedy for the little boy: To be six and already burned with a brand that never goes away in a small country school. But the fear, the fear of removal simply because you are different, is always there when you are

This article originally appeared in *The Safety Net* (1993), 4(1), pp. 2–3, and is reprinted by permission.

seven. It doesn't go away. This fear that it could be me next. This fear is confusing and breeds anger because there is no resolution to this fear.

This is the fear my son learned from his public education regular classroom.

A month before the boy was removed from Joey's classroom, I asked Joey what he thought about all this stuff. Was it okay to have kids who looked or talked differently in his class? Our conversation went something like this:

Me: So Joe, are there any kids in your class in wheelchairs?

Joey: No, but there was a girl last year.

Me: In a wheelchair?

Joey: Yeah, I pushed her around in the gym.

Me: She was in your kindergarten class?

Joey: Yeah.

Me: Was she nice?

Joey: Yeah, she was okay. She was fun to push. She liked it, I think, 'cause she laughed and stuff.

Me: She did stuff with the rest of the kids?

Joey: Yeah, but she is gone this year.

Me: Where did she go?

Joey: I don't know. She is just not in my class.

Me: Oh, that's too bad.

Joey: Yeah.

Two days after the boy I mentioned previously was removed from Joey's class, our conversation went something like this:

Me: Joey, I've been talking to teachers and other people about what you told me about how you thought having kids in your class who use a wheelchair is okay. I think that is a good thing to have everyone in the same class. Even kids who look different. Remember, we talked about this stuff.

Joey: Yeah.

Me: I'm proud of what you said.

Joey: Yeah.

Me: What are you thinking?

Joey:	Nothing.
Me:	What is it?
Joey:	Well, half my brain says something now.
Me:	Oh yeah, what does half of your brain say now?
Joey:	Half of my brain says I'm scared of those kids.
Me:	What kids?
Joey:	Those kids in wheelchairs.
Me:	Why?
Joey:	It's just one side of my brain. The other side says it's okay.
Me:	Well, I hope both sides say it's okay again soon.
Joey:	Yeah.

It was at this moment that I realized my child was learning to fear diversity. I couldn't make the fear go away. It was out of my control. No hug could make it all better. I was witnessing a loss of innocence.

I removed myself to another room and I cried.

2

Contemplating Inclusive Education from a Historical Perspective

William Stainback and Susan Stainback

For practically all of the history of civilization, education has been for the elite, and educational practices have reflected an elitist orientation (Blankenship and Lilly 1981).

Attempts to include all students in the mainstream of education, however, have persisted throughout history. In the United States, the great majority of students considered disabled learners were not deemed worthy of education at all until about the year 1800. Institutionalized, segregated education was the norm during the 19th century and much of the 20th century. Recent years have witnessed a movement toward mainstream education for many previously segregated learners, a movement sometimes slow and hesitant, but always progressive. Although progress has been hard won, the goal of universal mainstream education is potentially within the grasp of schools in the United States.

Education in the Early Years of the United States

For most students considered poor, minority, or disabled in colonial America, the first hurdle was merely to receive an education; integration into the mainstream of education would come much later. As early as 1779, Thomas Jefferson proposed the first state-supported school system to help provide an education to the poor of Virginia. Unfortunately, his plan was rejected. As stated by Sigmon (1983): "Indeed, in a society of class distinctions, the failure of the plan was undoubtedly caused by the refusal of well-to-do citizens to pay taxes for the education of the poor" (p. 5).

About a century after Jefferson's endeavor, however, the efforts of educational leaders such as Horace Mann, coupled with the massive influx of immigrants needing to be "Americanized" during the late 1800s and early 1900s, persuaded the affluent that the education of the "lower" classes was in their best interest. As a result, the states one by one adopted publicly supported education, all of them passing compulsory education attendance laws between 1842 and 1918.

All was not positive, however. Many blacks and Native Americans received no education, and those who did attended classes in a separate system of education. Similarly, students identified as disabled were generally unwelcome in the public schools. Tracking by academic ability became popular in schools, and poor and disadvantaged children routinely filled the lower, nonacademic tracks. Exceptions for early school leaving, primarily affecting children from the lower socioeconomic groups, were made. All of these actions worked against achieving a truly integrated mainstream education for all students.

Educating Persons with Disabilities

Benjamin Rush, a physician, was one of the first Americans to introduce the concept of educating persons with disabilities. Although Rush put forward the idea in the late 1700s, the first such educational program was not established until 1817, when Thomas Gallaudet opened the American Asylum for the Education and Instruction of the Deaf and Dumb in Connecticut. Other programs for educating students with various disabilities were established soon afterward. For example, the New England Asylum for the Education of the Blind was founded in 1829 in Watertown, Massachusetts, and the Experiential School for Teaching and Training Idiotic Children was founded in 1846 in Barre, Massachusetts. Still, not all students with disabilities received an education. Those who did often learned their lessons in asylums or government- or church-supported institutions. It was not until the mid-1800s that Samuel Howe advocated for the education of *all* children, an idea that, as discussed later in this chapter, did not emerge into actual practice until more than a century later, with the passage of PL 94-142 (now the Individuals with Disabilities Education Act, IDEA) by the U.S. Congress.

Even with the passage of compulsory attendance laws in the early 1900s, many children with disabilities continued to be excluded from the public schools. As Sigmon (1983, p. 3) notes, "almost all children who were wheelchair-bound, not toilet trained, or considered ineducable were excluded because of the problems that schooling them would entail." Further, those who were allowed to attend the schools were confronted by "a movement for the establishment of special classes. Special classes came about, not for humanitarian reasons but because such children were unwanted in the regular public school classroom. Feelings against . . . placing them in regular classrooms were strong" (Chaves 1977, p. 30). This is not meant to imply that individuals who have worked in special classes and special education throughout history have not had humanitarian motives.

Teachers in general education classrooms perceived educators working in special education classes as having special preparation or a special capacity for the work. Special education teachers were a breed apart, they said, and it was inappropriate to expect teachers lacking such preparation and inclination to participate in educating students in wheelchairs or students who have difficulty learning academics. This type of defensive and rejective reasoning led to the creation of what might be termed "little red schoolhouses for students considered exceptional" within regular school buildings. Students and teachers were "in" a regular school, but in many ways were not an accepted part of it. As special classes increased in number, attitudes among "general" and "special" educators and evolving administrative models for segregated education ensured that general and special education developed on parallel rather than converging lines.

While special classes and special day schools began to gain momentum in the early 1900s, educational programs in asylums and residential institutions for students with disabilities remained a dominant force, growing and expanding until the mid-1900s. In the 1950s and 1960s, special classes in public schools became the preferred educational delivery system for most students with disabilities; however, residential institutions and special schools remained the norm for educating students who were blind, deaf, and physically disabled. Over time, the situation was improving for some students with disabilities, but students considered severely or profoundly developmentally disabled were generally still denied educational services of any type, and they lived out their lives primarily in the wards of large state institutions.

Contributing to the lack of social and educational change was a common public perception that people with disabilities possessed criminal tendencies stemming from their genetic makeup (Davies 1930). Progress was hard won in the face of widespread public prejudice that individuals with disabilities had no place in ordinary school and community life.

Civil Rights and Public Education

In the 1950s and '60s, after the country had recovered from the hardships of a severe depression and two world wars, there developed an increased recognition and respect for the human dignity of all citizens, regardless of their individual differences. There was a powerful momentum away from more segregated options for the education of minority students. In the notable early landmark of this era, the 1954 *Brown v. Board of Education* decision, Chief Justice Warren (1954) ruled that "separate is not equal." While this ruling had an almost immediate effect in breaking down the exclusionary policies toward blacks and other racial and ethnic minorities, it also led the way toward the increased study of exclusionary policies for students with disabilities in later decades.

It was during the 1950s and '60s in the United States that parents of students with disabilities organized and initiated advocacy activities for educating their children, forming groups like the National Association for Retarded Citizens. A group of special education leaders, including

Burton Blatt (1969), Lloyd Dunn (1968), Gunnar Dybwad (1964), Nicholas Hobbs (1966), Stephen Lilly (1970), Maynard Reynolds (1962), and Wolf Wolfensberger (1972), had begun advocating for the right of students with disabilities to learn in a more normal school environment with their peers. For the first time, there was widespread agreement that the restrictions imposed by segregated settings such as institutions, special schools, and special classes were problematic.

Education in the Least Restrictive Environment

Although the 1950s and '60s saw increased support for mainstream education for the disabled, it was not until the 1970s that U.S. schools put into place the natural sequel to the 1954 *Brown v. Board of Education* decision for students with disabilities. Court decisions in Pennsylvania in 1971, and in the District of Columbia in 1972, established the right of all children labeled as mentally retarded to a free and appropriate education. These court rulings made it more difficult for students with disabilities to be excluded from the public schools and denied an education.

In 1973, Congress passed the Rehabilitation Act, Section 504, and later amendments that guaranteed the rights of persons with disabilities in employment and in educational institutions that receive federal monies. In 1975, due to pressure from parents, courts, and legislatures, Congress passed PL 94-142 (Education for All Handicapped Children Act). This law (now IDEA), enacted in 1978, stipulates that *no* child, regardless of disability, can be denied an appropriate public education in the least restrictive environment. It thus extended to all children the right to a free public education offered in the least segregated arrangement possible.

By 1976, all 50 states, spurred by the passage of PL 94-142, had passed laws subsidizing public school programs for students with disabilities. In addition, several national associations for regular educators passed resolutions in support of mainstreaming. Many states also began to require regular classroom teachers to take coursework to prepare them for mainstreaming. At about this same time, a number of people, most notably Norris Haring, Lou Brown, Wayne Sailor, Doug Guess, and William and Diane Bricker, began strongly advocating for the education of students with severe and profound disabilities in regular neighborhood schools. In 1979, the Association for Persons with Severe Handicaps adopted a resolution calling for the education of all students with severe disabilities in regular neighborhood schools with their nondisabled peers. A few years later, the national Society for Children and Adults with Autism adopted a similar resolution calling for the termination of segregated placements. Not until 1984, however, were the current dual systems of general and special education directly challenged by Susan and William Stainback in an article in the journal *Exceptional Children* in which they proposed the merger of special and regular education into one system of education designed to meet all students' needs (Stainback and Stainback 1984).

Educating All Students in General Education

By the late 1970s and early '80s, students considered mildly or moderately disabled were attending regular classes for at least part of the school day, and many students who had not been served in the past (those considered severely or profoundly disabled) increasingly began to receive educational services in regular neighborhood schools and to be part of such regular school environments as the cafeteria, playground, library, halls, buses, and restrooms (Certo, Haring, and York 1984; Knoblock 1982; Lusthaus 1988; Stainback and Stainback 1985; Stainback, Stainback, and Forest 1989; Villa and Thousand 1988).

In 1986, the U.S. Office of Special Education and Rehabilitation Services in the U.S. Department of Education issued the Regular Education Initiative (Will 1986), which incorporated some of the ideas of the Stainbacks in the 1984 proposal regarding the merger of special and general education into one unified system of education, but did not go as far as suggesting a total merger of the two systems. The purpose was to find ways to serve students with mild and moderate disabilities in regular classrooms by encouraging special education and other special programs to form a partnership with regular education. Margaret Wang, Jack Birch, and Maynard Reynolds, among others, have been strong supporters of the initiative (Reynolds and Birch 1988; Wang, Reynolds, and Walberg 1987).

By the mid- to late-1980s and early '90s, many educators and parents recognized the need to educate all students, not just those labeled mildly or moderately disabled, in the mainstream of regular education (Forest

1987; Knoblock 1982; Sapon-Shevin, Pugach, and Lilly 1987; Stainback and Stainback 1987, 1990, 1992a; Strully 1986; Thousand and Villa 1991; Villa and Thousand 1992). Parents and professional educators discussed and debated the merger of special and general education into one comprehensive regular education system (Gartner and Lipsky 1987, Stainback and Stainback 1984, York and Vandercook 1988, Villa and Thousand 1992). Some people began advocating for the part-time or full-time integration of students with severe and profound disabilities into the regular classroom, and some schools began experimenting with such integration (Forest 1987, Knoblock 1982, Stainback and Stainback 1988, Strully and Strully 1985, Thousand and Villa 1988). In 1988, the Association for Persons with Severe Handicaps adopted a resolution calling for the education of students with severe and profound disabilities in regular education and the integration of special and general education.

Despite the steady trend throughout U.S. history toward including all students in mainstream education, people have made many attempts to slow, stop, and even reverse this trend. Attempts to impede inclusion policies are evident even today. For instance, despite mandates for the placement of students in the least restrictive educational environments, some states have shown no progress in this area, and some have actually increased restrictive, segregated placements. Likewise, some states have made more rigid their categorical teacher certification, and some organizations and states have proposed the reinstitution of segregated schools for students with disabilities (Stainback and Stainback 1992b). Also, some scholars and researchers have argued against the integration movement (Fuchs and Fuchs 1994; Kauffman 1993; Kauffman, Gerber, and Semmel 1988; Lieberman 1988). As in the past, however, such arguments have done little to slow the overall trend toward achieving a mainstream education for students with disabilities.

During the past several years, the movement toward full inclusion of all students in the mainstream of general education has gained unparalleled momentum. Whereas a few years ago we saw only a handful of examples of full inclusion, today we see numerous examples of students with the most profound mental and physical disabilities participating successfully in mainstream classes in elementary and secondary schools. There's even an international organization whose mission is to promote full inclusion in schools; it is called Schools Are For Everyone, and it has thousands of members in the United States and other countries.

Discussions about inclusion have moved beyond the borders of special education circles. For example, leading general education journals such as *The Elementary School Journal* (Alper and Ryndak 1992) and *Educational Leadership* (Villa and Thousand 1992) have published articles on how full inclusion might be accomplished, and newspapers such as *USA Today* (Kelly 1993) and the *Wall Street Journal* (Lubman 1994) have published articles describing full inclusion to the general public.

The courts are increasingly being called upon to render judgements regarding full inclusion, the most recent and important being the *Oberti v. Clementon* (1993) decision in which U.S. Circuit Court Judge Edward R. Becker ordered the inclusion of a student with severe disabilities and wrote: "We construe IDEA's mainstreaming requirement to prohibit a school from placing a child with disabilities outside of a regular classroom if education of the child in the regular classroom, with supplementary aids and support services, can be achieved satisfactorily." In addition, the Office of Special Education and Rehabilitation Services in the U.S. Office of Education recently adopted policies encouraging inclusion of all students in the mainstream wherever and whenever possible. And a growing number of state departments of education are adopting policies that encourage and support inclusion (e.g., New Mexico State Department of Education).

Finally, in the 1990s, Villa and Thousand, among others, have helped put the inclusion movement in the context of general education reform (Thousand, Villa, and Nevin 1994; Villa and Thousand 1992). School restructuring[*] for all learners was addressed in 1992, with an ASCD resolution and a report from the National Association of State Boards of Education (see ASCD 1992, NASBE Study Group 1992). One of ASCD's six resolutions in 1992 was for the full inclusion of special programs through instructional environments that eliminate tracking and segregation, services that focus on the prevention of learning problems rather than after-the-fact labeling, minimal restrictive regulations, and flexible use of funding to promote success for all children. After two years of work, the NASBE study group published *Winners All: A Call for Inclusive Schools,* in which it recommended the creation of

---

[*]The remainder of this section on school restructuring was taken directly from Villa, R., J. Thousand, H. Meyers, and A. Nevin. (1993). "Regular and Special Education Teacher and Administrator Perceptions of Heterogeneous Education." Unpublished manuscript. Burlington: University of Vermont.

a unified education system, with major changes in organizational and instructional practices, preservice and inservice personnel preparation, licensure, and funding.

In the 1990s, the number of schools attempting to realize the ASCD and NASBE visions of inclusive education grew rapidly. Literature emerged describing some of these schools (e.g., Villa, Thousand, Paolucci-Whitcomb, and Nevin 1990; Villa, Thousand, Stainback, and Stainback 1992) and the methods they employed to adapt curriculum and instruction, and to alter the traditional schooling paradigm (e.g., Stainback and Stainback 1990, 1992 a, b; Stainback, Stainback, and Forest 1989; Thousand, Villa, and Nevin 1994; Villa, Thousand, Stainback, and Stainback 1992).

In summary, the inclusion debate of the 1990s has expanded beyond special education and became part of a total school reform movement. In fact, while the special education community continued to debate full inclusion versus a continuum of placement (educational options), two leading general education organizations (ASCD and NASBE) had endorsed the creation of "heterogeneous" (Villa and Thousand 1988, p. 144) or inclusionary schools.

Breaking Down the Final Barrier

Society is gradually moving away from the segregationist practices of the past and toward providing all students an equal opportunity to have their educational needs met within the mainstream of general education. A major barrier to this goal, and one that is being recognized increasingly, is the continued operation of the dual systems of special and regular education (Gartner and Lipsky 1987, Stainback and Stainback 1984, Villa and Thousand 1992).

As noted by Ted Kennedy Jr. (1986, p. 6), it is those individuals identified as disabled who constitute the "last bastion of segregation." If this segregation can be broken down in the public school system and all students educated in the mainstream of general education, we will be well on the way to breaking down segregation in society in general.

References

Alper, S., and D. Ryndak. (1992). "Educating Students with Severe Handicaps in Regular Classes." *The Elementary School Journal* 92: 373–387.

ASCD. (1992). *Resolutions 1992*. Alexandria, Va.: Association for Supervision and Curriculum Development.

Blankenship, C., and S. Lilly. (1981). *Mainstreaming Students with Learning and Behavior Problems*. New York: Holt, Rinehart and Winston.

Blatt, B. (1969). *Exodus from Pandemonium*. Boston: Allyn and Bacon.

Certo, N., N. Haring, and R. York, eds. (1984). *Public School Integration of Severely Handicapped Students*. Baltimore, Md.: Paul H. Brookes Publishing.

Chaves, I.M. (1977). "Historical Overview of Special Education in the United States. In *Mainstreaming: Problems, Potentials and Perspectives*, edited by P. Bates, T.L. West, and R.B. Schmerl. Minneapolis: National Support Systems Project.

Davies, S.P. (1930). *Social Control of the Mentally Deficient*. New York: Thomas Y. Crowell Co.

Dunn, L.M. (1968). "Special Education for the Mildly Retarded—Is Much of It Justifiable?" *Exceptional Children* 35, 1: 5–22.

Dybwad, G. (1964). *Challenges in Mental Retardation*. New York: Columbia University Press.

Forest, M. (November 1987). "Start with the Right Attitude." *Entourage* 2: 11–13.

Forest, M., and E. Lusthaus. (1987). "The Kaleidoscope: A Challenge to the Cascade." *More Education Integration*, edited by M. Forest. Toronto, Ontario: G. Allan Roeher Institute.

Fuchs, D., and L. Fuchs. (1994). "Inclusive Schools Movement and the Radicalization of Special Education Reform." *Exceptional Children* 60: 294–309.

Gartner, A., and D. Lipsky. (1987). "Beyond Special Education." *Harvard Educational Review* 57: 367–395.

Goldberg, I., and W.M. Cruickshank. (1958). "The Trainable but Noneducable: Whose Responsibility?" *National Education Association Journal* 47: 622.

Hobbs, N. (1966). "Helping the Disturbed Child: Psychological and Ecological Strategies." *American Psychologist* 21: 1,105–1,115.

Kauffman, J. (1993). "How We Might Achieve the Radical Reform of Special Education." *Exceptional Children* 60: 294–309.

Kauffman, J., M. Gerber, and M. Semmel. (1988). "Arguable Assumptions Underlying the Regular Education Initiative." *Journal of Learning Disabilities* 21, 1: 6–11.

Kelly, D. (April 21, 1993). "Can Inclusion Be an Intrusion? Kids with Disabilities Enter Regular Classroom." *USA Today*, sec. D, p. 7.

Kennedy Jr., T. (November 23, 1986). "Our Right to Independence." *Parade Magazine*, pp. 4–7.

Knoblock, P. (1982). *Teaching and Mainstreaming Autistic Children*. Denver: Love Publishing Co.

Lieberman, L. (1988). *Preserving Special Education for Those Who Need It*. Newtonville, Mass.: GloWorm Publications.

Lilly, S. (1970). "Special Education: A Tempest in a Teapot." *Exceptional Children* 32: 43–49.

Lubman, S. (April 13, 1994). "More Schools Embrace Full Inclusion of the Disabled." *Wall Street Journal*, sec. B, p. 1.

Lusthaus, E. (1988). "Education Integration . . . Letting Our Children Go." *Journal of the Association for the Severely Handicapped* 14: 6–7.

NASBE Study Group on Special Education. (October 1992). *Winners All: Call for Inclusive Schools*. Alexandria, Va: National Association of State Boards of Education.

Oberti v. Clementon. (1993). Rafael Oberti v. Board of Education of Clementon, New Jersey (no. 92-5462, 3rd Cir. 5/28/93, Becker, J.)

Reynolds, M. (1962). "Framework for Considering Some Issues in Special Education." *Exceptional Children* 28: 367–370.

Reynolds, M.C., and J.W. Birch. (1988). *Adaptive Mainstreaming*. New York: Longman.

Sapon-Shevin, M., M. Pugach, and S. Lilly. (November 1987). *Moving Toward Merger: Implications for General and Special Education*. Paper presented at the tenth annual Teacher Education Division of the Council for Exceptional Children Conference, Arlington, Va.

Sigmon, S. (1983). "The History and Future of Educational Segregation." *Journal for Special Educators* 19: 1–13.

Stainback, S., and W. Stainback. (1988). "Educating Students with Severe Disabilities in Regular Classes." *Teaching Exceptional Children* 21: 16–19.

Stainback, S., and W. Stainback. (1990). *Support Networks for Inclusive Schooling*. Baltimore: Paul H. Brookes.

Stainback, S., and W. Stainback. (1992a). *Curriculum Considerations for Inclusive Classrooms*. Baltimore: Paul H. Brookes.

Stainback, S., W. Stainback, and M. Forest. (1989). *Educating All Students in the Mainstream of Regular Education*. Baltimore: Paul H. Brookes.

Stainback, W., and S. Stainback. (1984). "A Rationale for the Merger of Special and Regular Education. *Exceptional Children* 51: 102–111.

Stainback, W., and S. Stainback. (1985). *Integration of Students with Severe Disabilities into Regular Education*. Reston, Va.: Council for Exceptional Children.

Stainback, W., and S. Stainback. (1987). "Educating All Students in Regular Education. *The Association for Severely Handicapped Newsletter* 13, 4: 1, 7.

Stainback, W., and S. Stainback. (1992b). *Controversial Issues Confronting Special Education*. Boston: Allyn and Bacon.

Strully, J. (1986). *Our Children and the Regular Education Classroom: Or Why Settle for Anything Less than the Best?* Paper presented to the 1986 annual conference of the Association for Persons with Severe Handicaps, San Francisco.

Strully, J., and C. Strully. (1985). "Teach Your Children." *Canadian Journal on Mental Retardation* 35, 4: 3–11.

Thousand, J., and R. Villa. (1988). "Enhancing Educational Success Through Collaboration." *IMPACT* 1: 14.

Thousand, J., and R. Villa. (1991). "A Futuristic View of the REI: A Response to Jenkins, Pious, and Jewell." *Exceptional Children* 57: 556–562.

Thousand, J., R. Villa., and A. Nevin. (1994). *Creativity and Collaborative Learning: A Practical Guide to Empowering Students and Teachers.* Baltimore: Paul H. Brookes.

Villa, R. (1989). "Model Public School Inservice Programs: Do They Exist? *Teacher Education and Special Education* 12: 173–176.

Villa, R., and J. Thousand. (1988). "Enhancing Success in Heterogeneous Classrooms and Schools: The Powers of Partnership." *Teacher Education and Special Education* 11: 144–154.

Villa, R., and J. Thousand, J. (October 1992). "How One District Integrated Special and Regular Education." *Educational Leadership* 50, 2: 39–41.

Villa, R., J. Thousand, P. Paolucci-Whitcomb, and A. Nevin. (1990). "In Search of New Paradigms for Collaborative Consultation." *Journal of Educational and Psychological Consultation* 1: 279–292.

Villa, R., J. Thousand, W. Stainback, and S. Stainback. (1992). *Restructuring for Caring and Effective Education: An Administrative Guide to Creating Heterogeneous Schools.* Baltimore: Paul H. Brookes.

Wang, M., M. Reynolds, and H.J. Walberg. (1987). *Handbook of Special Education Research and Practice.* Oxford, England: Pergamon.

Warren, E. (1954). *Brown v. Board of Education of Topeka,* 347 U.S. 483, 493.

Will, M. (1986). *Educating Students with Learning Problems—A Shared Responsibility.* Washington, D.C.: U.S. Department of Education, Office of Special Education and Rehabilitation Services.

Wolfensberger, W. (1972). *The Principle of Normalization in Human Services.* Toronto, Ontario: National Institute on Mental Retardation.

York, J., and T. Vandercook. (1988). Feature issue on integrated education. *IMPACT* 1: 1–3.

3

The Rationales for Creating Inclusive Schools

Richard A. Villa and Jacqueline S. Thousand

The Goals of Public Education

Various rationales support the growing movement advocating for the creation of inclusionary, or heterogeneous, schools. We'd like to begin an exploration of these rationales by inviting you to think about and answer the following question: What should be the goals of public education? In other words, what outcomes, attitudes, dispositions, and skills do you want the children you care about to possess by the time they leave high school? After you have answered this question from your personal and professional perspective, try answering it from the perspective of others—students with and without identified disabilities, and adults with roles or concerns in education that are different from your own (e.g., a parent, an educator, an administrator, a local

* We gratefully acknowledge the support and suggestions of Vince Ercolano with respect to the writing of this chapter.

businessperson, a community member). Do your responses have commonalities?

Over the past decade, we have posed this question to tens of thousands of parents, teachers, administrators, students, university professors, and concerned citizens of the United States, Bermuda, Canada, Honduras, Micronesia, the Czech Republic, Slovakia, China, and Russia. Regardless of the divergent perspectives, vested interests, or locale of the respondents, their answers are very similar and tend to fall into one or more of the four categories shown in Figure 3.1—*belonging, mastery, independence,* and *generosity*—which have been borrowed from Native American culture.

FIGURE 3.1

Frequently Identified Goals of Public Education by Category

Belonging
 Having friends
 Being able to form and maintain relationships
 Getting along with others, including coworkers
 Being part of a community
 Being a caring parent and family member

Mastery
 Having success and becoming competent in something or some things
 Being well-rounded
 Being a good problem solver
 Being flexible
 Being motivated
 Being literate
 Being able to use technology
 Being a lifelong learner
 Reaching potential in areas of interest

Independence
 Having choices in work, recreation, leisure, or continued learning
 Being confident to take risks
 Being as independent as possible
 Assuming personal responsibility
 Being accountable for actions and decisions
 Being able to self-advocate

Generosity
 Being a contributing member of society
 Valuing diversity
 Being empathetic
 Offering compassion, caring, and support to others
 Being a responsible citizen
 Being a global steward

Traditional Native American education was based on the culture's main purpose for existence—the education and empowerment of its children. The educational philosophy and approach were holistic, with the central goal being to foster a child's "Circle of Courage" (Brendtro, Brokenleg, and Van Bockern 1990, p. 34). The circle consisted of the four educational objectives or components of self-esteem cited here.

Thus, although the people sampled are diverse, they share common beliefs as to the desired outcomes for students. Furthermore, these outcomes are the same for children with identified educational, physical, social, and emotional challenges as for children who never are labeled "special" in some way. Examining the outcomes of education listed under each goal in Figure 3.1, it becomes clear that people believe that the curriculum must include, but also go far beyond, traditional academic domains. The curriculum must address the concerns so poignantly expressed in Ginott's letter to teachers (see Figure 3.2).

Historically, much of what has been done in the name of "special education" has compromised or mitigated against students' opportu-

---

FIGURE 3.2
Letter to Teachers

Dear Teacher,

I am a survivor of a concentration camp. My eyes saw what no man should witness.

Gas chambers built by learned engineers.
Children poisoned by educated physicians.
Infants killed by trained nurses.
Women and babies shot and burned by high school and college graduates.

So I am suspicious of education.
My request is: Help your students become human.
Your efforts must never produce learned monsters, skilled psychopaths,
    educated Eichmanns.
Reading, writing, arithmetic are important only if they serve to make our children
    more humane.

Source: H. Ginott. *Teacher and Child* (New York: Macmillan, 1972).
Reprinted by permission.

nity to attain the components of the Circle of Courage. Specifically, in an effort to focus on students' skill development to promote *independence*, we have sent them to "specialized" instruction in separate environments. And although it is important for students to develop skills and independence, it is difficult for them to feel they *belong* when they are sent down the hall or to a different school to develop those skills. Contemporary motivational theorists (e.g., Brendtro et al. 1990, Glasser 1986, Maslow 1970) stress the fulfillment of a child's need to belong as critical, if not prerequisite, to a child's motivation to learn. Exclusion or removal of a child from regular education, on the other hand, instructs the child that *belonging* is not forthcoming—that it is not a basic human right but something that must be earned. Norman Kunc (1992) describes the dilemma:

> The tragic irony . . . is that as soon as we take away students' sense of belonging, we completely undermine their capacity to learn the skills that will enable them to belong. Herein lies the most painful "Catch-22" situation that confronts students with disabilities—they can't belong until they learn, but they can't learn because they are prevented from belonging (p. 35).

Changing Assumptions

We know that schooling must be based on assumptions about *future* society and the skills, attitudes, and dispositions that will be needed for success in that society. Yet, in many communities, schools are organized to respond to assumptions about life in the 19th and early 20th centuries. That is, they are attempting to provide an excellent education for the elite, Americanize new immigrant populations, and otherwise track children for stratified work roles in a relatively static factory economy in which query, creative problem solving, and collaboration are not wanted or needed. Other school communities unconsciously (or consciously) still attempt to promote a common, homogeneous culture (i.e., the white, Anglo-Saxon, Protestant, rural culture of the 1800s).

Change, clearly, can be scary and difficult; and the status quo often wins out over fundamental change. In education, the status quo has been maintained, at least in part, by "sending away" every child who fails to learn from (or is not challenged by) educational approaches based on the 19th and 20th century assumptions just described. An exciting result of the exploration of mismatches between educational assumptions and practice is the *change* that occurs in how we think about children with disabilities.

Educators who understand the curriculum for the 21st century and who have risked and succeeded in educating children with disabilities in general education know and will argue that children with disabilities are a gift to educational reform. These children force us to "bust the paradigm" of traditional schooling and try new things, so that we are more capable of meeting their unique needs *and those of many other students.* When very diverse populations of students are welcomed as members of a school community, standardization, assimilation, and sorting or tracking can no longer drive or characterize "effective education." The changes in curricular, instructional, and organizational practices that are introduced (e.g., cooperative group learning; student-directed learning; active participation; detracking; a focus on social skills and communication competence; community service) better prepare *every* student for the future—a future that is already here.

Efficacy Data

Question: "What is the number one method for assessing student performance in the United States?"

Answer: "Norm-referenced standardized achievement tests."

Question: "If we agree with educational futurists and the many thousands of people who identified belonging, mastery, independence, and generosity as important goals of education, what are the standardized achievement tests we use to measure our children's performance in these goal areas?"

Answer: "There aren't any."

In education, we do not always measure what we say we value or consider critical for our children's success. But shouldn't we? As Vito Perrone suggests in *Expanding Student Assessment* (1991), we can figure out how to measure anything of value to us if we simply consider developing and using something other than norm-referenced standardized assessments. Perrone recommends using *authentic assessments* that "get closer to student learning and are related to performance and understanding" (p. viii).

In the employment arena, the data available for graduates of separate special education programs suggest high levels of unemployment (over 50 percent one year after graduation) and underemployment

(Wagner 1989). In contrast, Ferguson and Asch (1989) found that the more time children with disabilities spent in regular classes, the more they achieved as adults in employment and continuing education. This held true regardless of gender, race, socioeconomic status (SES), type of disability, or the age at which the child gained access to general education. Research reviews and meta-analyses known as the special education "efficacy studies" (Lipsky and Gartner 1989, p. 19) showed that placement outside of general education had little or no positive effects for students regardless of the intensity or type of disability. In a review of three meta-analyses that looked at the most effective setting for educating students with special needs, Baker, Wang, and Walberg (1994) concluded that "special-needs students educated in regular classes do better academically and socially than comparable students in noninclusive settings" (p. 34). Their review yielded the same results regardless of the type of disability or grade level.

Regarding students with severe disabilities, Hollowood, Salisbury, Rainforth, and Palombaro (1995) found their inclusion was not detrimental to classmates. Others found their inclusion enhanced classmates' (Costello 1991, Kaskinen-Chapman 1992) as well as their own learning (e.g., Cole and Meyer 1991, Strain 1983, Straub and Peck 1994) and yielded social and emotional benefits for all students, with self-esteem and attendance improving for some students considered "at risk" (Kelly 1992).

Finally, as Kozol (1991) and others remind us, a gross overrepresentation of minorities in special education suggests a racist aspect of continuing separate programs. For example, African American children are three times more likely to be placed in special education classes than are European American children, and only half as likely to be placed in advanced or gifted programs (Scherer 1992–1993).

In summary, as Lipsky and Gartner (1989) observed,

> The basic premise of special education was that students with deficits will benefit from a unique body of knowledge and from smaller classes staffed by specially trained teachers using special materials. But there is no compelling body of evidence demonstrating that segregated special education programs have significant benefits for students (p. 19).

Legal Issues

In response to the current increase in advocacy for the inclusion of children with disabilities in general education, many ask whether the law regarding the education of children with disabilities has recently changed. The answer, of course, is no. Since the Education of All Handicapped Children Act was promulgated in 1975, the law and subsequent reauthorizations—including the 1989 amendment that changed the law's title to Individuals with Disabilities Education Act (IDEA)—have reflected Congress's preference for educating children with disabilities in regular classrooms with their peers. Specifically, under 20 U.S.C. Section 1412(5)(B), each state must have procedures to ensure that children with disabilities are removed from the regular educational environment only when the nature or severity of the disability is such that education in regular classes cannot be achieved satisfactorily with the use of supplementary aids and services.

So, then, it is not the law that has changed. Instead, it is the know-how of teachers, administrators, and communities that has changed as a consequence of "doing it" (Cross and Villa 1992). The change has come in the form of an emerging competence and confidence of educational personnel, together with the organizational, instructional, curricular, and technological advancements they have developed to meaningfully educate students with significant challenges within general education. The observed student success, contrasted with the lackluster results of former segregated special education programs, has heightened the expectations and motivation of families and educators to rethink past practices and publicly advocate for opportunities for children with disabilities to belong to their local general education community.

Since 1975, federal court cases have clarified the intent of the law in favor of the inclusion of children with disabilities in general education. For example, in 1983, *Roncker v. Walter* addressed the issue of "bringing educational services to the child" versus "bringing the child to the services." The case was resolved in favor of integrated versus segregated placement and established a *principle of portability;* that is, "if a desirable service currently provided in a segregated setting can feasibly be delivered in an integrated setting, it would be inappropriate under PL 94-142 to provide the service in a segregated environment" (700 F. 2d at 1063). The 1988 U.S. Court of Appeals ruling in favor of Timothy W., a student with severe disabilities whose school district contended he was "too disabled" to be entitled to an education, clarified school districts' responsibility to educate all children and specified that the term *all* included in IDEA meant *all* children with disabilities, without exception. In 1993, the U.S. Court of Appeals for the Third Circuit upheld the right of Rafael Oberti, a boy with Down syndrome, to receive his education in his neighborhood regular school with adequate and necessary supports, placing the burden of proof for compliance with IDEA's mainstreaming requirements squarely on the school district and the state rather than on the family. In 1994, the U.S. Court of Appeals for the Ninth Circuit upheld the district court decision in *Holland v. Sacramento Unified School District* in which Judge David S. Levi indicated that when school districts place students with disabilities, the *presumption and starting point is the mainstream.* It is noteworthy that the Clinton administration via the Office of Special Education Programs filed a "friend of the court" brief with the Court of Appeals in support of Rachel Holland's placement in general education.

Procedural Issues

An estimated 35 to 50 percent of special educators' time nationally is devoted to assessment and other documentation related to students' Individual Educational Plans (IEPs) (Vermont Department of Education 1990). Unfortunately, much of the assessment conducted yields little diagnostic information to help educators with instruction. Instead, it enables them to comply with the legal requirement to categorize students as "apples, oranges, or potatoes." Given the widely varying eligibility criteria from one state to the next, particularly in the area of learning disabilities, Ysseldyke (1987) concluded that on any given day more than 80 percent of a school's student body could be classified as learning disabled. Even if labels were consistently valid and reliable, no evidence suggests that all children given a particular global label (e.g., autistic, Down syndrome, emotional behavioral disorder, learning disabled, severely disabled, talented and gifted) learn in the same way, are motivated by the same things, or have the same gifts or challenges. As teachers intuitively know, homogeneity among children is a myth.

None of the huge amount of special education paperwork holds teachers accountable for student learning. Nowhere in the interpretation of IDEA is it stated or expected that educators be held accountable for student progress. Instead, the paperwork (e.g., timelines, notices of meetings, comprehensive reports, annual reviews of IEPs) represents procedural "proxy" measures of actual student change. So, all of this time spent on paperwork doesn't necessarily promote quality programming for children. Yet, as Madeline Hunter notes (personal communication, August 15, 1986), "To say that I am an effective teacher, and acknowledge that my students may not be learning is the same as saying I am a great surgeon, but most of my patients die."

The procedures that have mushroomed over two decades of attempting to implement IDEA clearly have focused on the wrong things—proxy measures of progress and "voodoo" (i.e., unreliable, invalid, instructionally uninforming) assessment procedures and outcomes. For some, including parents, special educators, and advocates, procedural issues have been enough to fire a call for change in an educational system that labels and segregates nearly half of our children based on educationally questionable assessment instruments and student monitoring procedures.

Population Increases

A major concern—particularly for special educators who must assess and then serve the students identified as having disabilities—is the rising number of children eligible for special education. For instance, the number of students eligible for special education increased 23 percent from FY 77 to FY 90 (Fuchs and Fuchs 1994). In the decade from 1977 to 1987, the number of children labeled "learning disabled" alone increased 119 percent (Lipsky and Gartner 1989). Some of these increases can be accounted for by North American educational practices that far too long provided insufficient or no services for students with even mild disabilities. However, the staggering and continuing annual increase is so out of hand that nationally "nearly 50 percent of our students receive services from or are eligible for a variety of special programs serving students with disabilities, economic or social disadvantages, special talents, etc." (Vermont Department of Education 1993, p. 1). Given this fact, we must stop and ask ourselves, "Is the disability in the child, or is the disability in the educational system we have created?"

Disjointedness

Much discussion has focused on the dual systems of general and special education. In reality, we do not have dual systems but multiple systems of education. Aside from general and special education, there is adult education, vocational education, gifted education, rural education, bilingual education, English as a second language (ESL) education, at-risk education, and more. As pointed out earlier, it is increasingly difficult for any child to be eligible solely for regular education. Of course, all of these programs, in their inception, are well intended. The problem is that they were separately launched, in a disjointed and incremental fashion, with their own eligibility criteria, funding formulas, and advocacy groups. That so many "special" programs have been created for so many children suggests that general education, as currently conceptualized and organized, is failing an increasing proportion of children.

Funding

Costs associated with the exclusion of children can be significant in dollar terms as well as in other human terms. For example, for FY 94 the federal government expended more than $2.5 billion on special education, while local school districts spent $3 billion—in addition to general busing costs to transport children with disabilities to special education placements, primarily away from their local schools (Hehir 1994). The anticipated cost of educating children with disabilities in local school general education was an argument in the early 1980s for why inclusive education would not be possible. Since then, communities across the country have demonstrated that educating all children in local school regular education classrooms does not necessarily cost more. In some cases, the reduction in busing costs and the elimination of duplicate services have saved dollars that then could be used to enrich instructional resources in local general education classrooms, thus benefiting many more children.

Interestingly, some opponents of inclusion have criticized the citing of potential cost savings from returning children "home" as inappropriate, if not unethical. We agree that inclusion should not be "sold" for financial reasons alone; we always must advocate for what is best for children. However, there is nothing wrong with being fiscally responsible. As already noted, education often has squandered its resources through poor coordination and communication among programs, service providers, and advocacy efforts.

State formulas for funding special education also have created barriers to progress toward more inclusive education. Many state funding formulas provide fiscal incentives for serving children with special needs in separate or segregated classrooms and programs. For example, in Texas, the state funding formula for special education pays local school districts 10 times more money for instructing students in separate versus regular classrooms. As a result, Texas has the lowest percentage of students in the country (5 percent) receiving an education in regular classrooms. In contrast, in 1988 Vermont changed to a "fiscally neutral" funding formula that offers no incentives or disincentives for placing children with disabilities in regular classrooms and allows dollars to follow children rather than be designated to particular programs or places. In 1993, five years after the law's enactment, 83 percent of Vermont's children eligible for special education were educated in regular classes. Fiscal Year 94 saw 19 additional states reviewing and considering reform of their special education funding formulas.

Philosophy

A compelling rationale for educational reform is that categorical segregation of any subgroup of people is simply a violation of civil rights and the principle of "equal citizenship." Many believe what Chief Justice Earl Warren (1954) clarified in the landmark *Brown v. Board of Education* decision over four decades ago, that is, that separateness in education can

> generate a feeling of inferiority as to [children's] status in the community that may affect their hearts and minds in a way unlikely ever to be undone. This sense of inferiority . . . affects the motivation of a child to learn . . . [and] has a tendency to retard . . . educational and mental development (p. 493).

Many advocates of inclusive education see the parallels to other struggles for human and civil rights and recall images of administrators of the 1950s and '60s blocking "white" schoolhouse doors to keep out African American children. They are saddened by the fact that in far too many communities, school officials still block the doors, but this time to keep out children with disabilities. They know that the number one determinant of whether or not a child with disabilities has access to regular education is *where* the child's family happens to live. They experience how arbitrary and unfair this situation is, as did a mother, who, after three years of battling for her daughter's admission into regular education, observed that "the Berlin Wall is down, Nelson Mandela has been released, but Molly still has not attended her neighborhood school" (Wessels 1992, p. 285).

Demonstrations and Recognition

"More is learned from a single success than from multiple failures. A single success proves it can be done—whatever is, is possible" (Klopf 1979, p. 40).

"By the fall of 1993 almost every state was implementing inclusion at some level" (Webb 1994, p.2).

Schools implementing inclusion are attempting to educate an increasingly diverse student body and include students with disabilities in local regular class and community environments. Such demonstrations help to change the line of questioning from "Can such a thing be done?" to "How can we learn from the examples and make it work in our unique community?"

Recognition of a mounting momentum and national movement in support of inclusive educational practices can have an additional influence on some people. The thinking is that, "Well, if these leaders and this mass of people consider this a viable and valuable path to take, perhaps we should consider it for our community." Observers in this category might be influenced by the fact that three prominent general educational organizations in the United States—the Association for Supervision and Curriculum Development (1992), the Council of Chief State School Officers (1992), and the National Association of State Boards of Education (1992)—have studied and authored position papers in support of policies and practices for inclusive schooling. Observers also may be influenced by emerging data supporting inclusion from both special and regular educators. For example, in a multistate study of 680 education professionals *experienced* in inclusive practices, both regular and special education professionals favored educating children with disabilities in general education through a shared collaborative relationship among general and special educators. Both groups also perceived benefits for educators and children (Thousand, Villa, Meyers, and Nevin 1994). The study substantiated findings of previous research (Cross and Villa 1992; Neary, Halvorsen, Kronberg, and Kelly 1992; Salisbury, Palombaro, and Hollowood 1993; Thousand, Fox, Reid, Godek, Williams, and Fox 1986; Villa, Thousand, Stainback, and Stainback 1992; Williams, Fox, Thousand, and Fox 1990) that identified the following as necessary supports for inclusive schooling:

• ongoing administrative support and leadership to promote a vision and practice of inclusive education;

• a culture and climate of caring and community;

• shared decision making and collaboration among regular and special educators, students, families, and other school personnel;

• time for collaboration; and

• ongoing inservice training and technical assistance to develop educators' competence in heterogeneous educational practices.

Which Rationale Is Most Compelling for You?

Figure 3.3 represents a "concept map" of the 10 rationales for change described in this chapter. We invite you to examine the figure and reread sections of this chapter that clarify any of the rationales. With these rationales in mind, we then invite you to respond to the following questions:

• Personally and professionally, which of the rationales are most compelling to you; that is, which are most likely to lead you to reject continued segregation of general and special education and instead support a unified, inclusive educational system?

• Which of the rationales would your colleagues, supervisors, students, community members, and policymakers find most compelling?

Your answers to these two questions are important to a discussion in the next chapter of how beliefs and attitudes can be influenced to support inclusion.

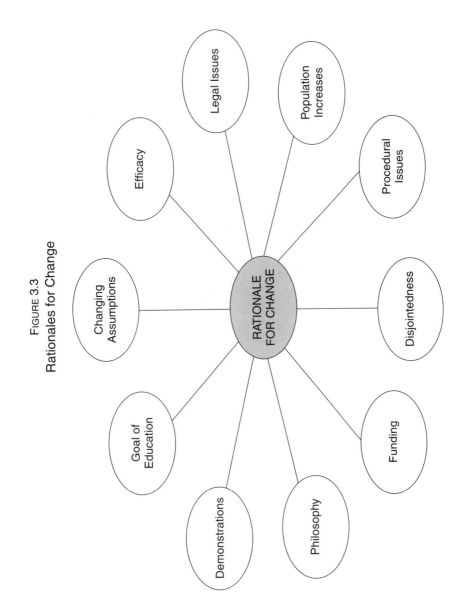

Figure 3.3
Rationales for Change

References

Association for Supervision and Curriculum Development. (1992). *Resolutions 1991.* Alexandria, Va.: Author.

Baker, E., M. Wang, and H. Walberg. (1994). "The Effects of Inclusion on Learning." *Educational Leadership* 52, 4: 33–35.

Brendtro, L., M. Brokenleg, and S. Van Bockern. (1990). *Reclaiming Youth at Risk: Our Hope for the Future.* Bloomington, Ind.: National Educational Service.

Cole, D.A. and L.H. Meyer. (1991). "Social Integration and Severe Disabilities: A Longitudinal Analysis of Child Outcomes." *The Journal of Special Education* 25: 340–351.

Costello, C. (1991). "A Comparison of Student Cognitive and Social Achievement for Handicapped and Regular Education Students Who Are Educated in Integrated Versus a Substantially Separate Classroom." Unpublished doctoral diss., University of Massachusetts, Amherst.

Council of Chief State School Officers. (1992). "Special Education and School Restructuring." *Concerns* (Issue 35): 1–7.

Cross, G., and R. Villa. (1992). "The Winooski School System: An Evolutionary Perspective of a School Restructuring for Diversity." In *Restructuring for Caring and Effective Education,* edited by R. Villa, J. Thousand, W. Stainback, and S. Stainback. Baltimore: Paul H. Brookes.

Ferguson, P., and A. Asch. (1989). "Lessons from Life: Personal and Parental Perspectives on School, Childhood, and Disability." In *Disability and Society* (pp. 108–140), edited by D. Biklen, A. Ford, and D. Ferguson. Chicago: National Society for the Study of Education.

Fuchs, D., and L.S. Fuchs. (1994). "Inclusive Schools Movement and the Radicalization of Special Education Reform." *Exceptional Children* 60, 4: 294–309.

Ginott, H. (1972). *Teacher and Child.* New York: Macmillan.

Glasser, W. (1986). *Control Theory in the Classroom.* New York: Harper & Row.

Hehir, T. (1994). "Toward a Better Outcome for Students with Disabilities." Paper presented at the Mid-Winter Conference of the Texas Council of Administrators of Special Education, Austin, Tex.

Hollowood, T., C. Salisbury, B. Rainforth, and M. Palombaro. (1995). "Use of Instructional Time in Classrooms Serving Students with and Without Severe Disabilities." *Exceptional Children* 61, 3: 242–253.

Hunter, M. Personal communication, August 15, 1986.

Kaskinen-Chapman, A. (1992). "Saline Area Schools and Inclusive Community Concepts." In *Restructuring for Caring and Effective Education: An Administrative Guide to Creating Heterogeneous Schools,* edited by R. Villa, J. Thousand, W. Stainback, and S. Stainback. Baltimore: Paul H. Brookes.

Kelly, D. (1992). "Introduction." In *Curricular Adaptations for Inclusive Classrooms,* edited by T. Neary, A. Halvorsen, R. Kronberg, and D. Kelly. San

Francisco: California Research Institute for the Integration of Students with Severe Disabilities, San Francisco State University.

Klopf, G.J. (1979). *The Principal and Staff Development in the School—With a Special Focus on the role of the Principal in Mainstreaming.* New York: Bank Street College of Education.

Kozol, J. (1991). *Savage Inequalities: Children in America's Schools.* New York: Harper Collins Publishers.

Kunc, N. (1992). "The Need to Belong: Rediscovering Maslow's Hierarchy of Needs." In *Restructuring for Caring and Effective Education: An Administrative Guide to Creating Heterogeneous Schools,* edited by R. Villa, J. Thousand, W. Stainback, and S. Stainback. Baltimore: Paul H. Brookes.

Lipsky, D., and A. Gartner. (1989). *Beyond Separate Education: Quality Education for All.* Baltimore: Paul H. Brookes.

Maslow, A. (1970). *Motivation and Personality.* New York: Harper & Row.

National Association of State Boards of Education Study Group on Special Education. (1992). *Winners All: A Call for Inclusive Schools.* Alexandria, Va.: Author.

Neary, T., A. Halvorsen, R. Kronberg, and D. Kelly. (1992). *Curricular Adaptations for Inclusive Classrooms.* San Francisco: California Research Institute for the Integration of Students with Severe Disabilities, San Francisco State University.

Perrone, V. (1991). *Expanding Student Assessment.* Alexandria, Va.: Association for Supervision and Curriculum Development.

Roncker v. Walter. (1983). 700 F.2d 1058, l063 (6th Circ.) cert. denied, 464 U.S. 864.

Salisbury, C., M. Palombaro, and T. Hollowood (1993). "On the Nature and Change of an Inclusionary Elementary School." *Journal of the Association for Persons with Severe Handicaps* 18, 2: 75–84.

Scherer, M. (1992–93). "On Savage Inequalities: A Conversation with Jonathan Kozol." *Educational Leadership* 50, 4: 4–9.

Strain, P. (1983). "Generalization of Autistic Children's Social Behavior Change: Effects of Developmentally Integrated and Segregated Settings." *Analysis and Intervention in Developmental Disabilities* 3, 1: 23–34.

Straub, D. and C. Peck. (1994). "What Are the Outcomes for Nondisabled Students? *Educational Leadership* 52, 4: 36–40.

Thousand, J., T. Fox, R. Reid, J. Godek, W. Williams, and W. Fox (1986). *The Homecoming Model: Educating Students Who Present Intensive Educational Challenges Within Regular Education Environments.* Monograph No. 7-1. Burlington: University of Vermont, Center for Developmental Disabilities.

Thousand, J., R. Villa, H. Meyers, and A. Nevin. (April 1994). "The Heterogeneous Education Teacher Survey: A Retrospective Analysis of Heterogeneous (Full Inclusion) Education." Paper presented ant the Annual Convention of the American Education Research Association, New Orleans.

Vermont Department of Education. (1990). *Report of the Special Commission on Special Education, State of Vermont.* Montpelier: Vermont Department of Education.

Vermont Department of Education. (1993). *Vermont Act 230: A Fourth Annual Meeting* (pp. 24–52). *Status Report on the Impact of Act 230.* Montpelier: Vermont Department of Education, Family and Education Support Team.

Villa, R., J. Thousand, W. Stainback, and S. Stainback. (1992). *Restructuring for Caring and Effective Education: An Administrative Guide to Creating Heterogeneous Schools.* Baltimore: Paul H. Brookes.

Wagner, M. (1989). "Youth with Disabilities During Transition: An Overview and Description of Findings from the National Longitudinal Transition Study." In *Transition Institute at Illinois: Project Director's Fourth Annual Meeting* (pp. 24–52), edited by J. Chadsey-Rusch. Champaign: University of Illinois.

Warren, E. (1954). *Brown v. Board of Education of Topeka,* 347 U.S. 483, 493.

Webb, N. (1994). "Special Education: With New Court Decisions Backing Them, Advocates See Inclusion as a Question of Values." *The Harvard Educational Letter* 10, 4: 1–3.

Wessels, M. (1992). "Building Community Support for Restructuring." In *Restructuring for Caring and Effective Education: An Administrative Guide to Creating Heterogeneous Schools,* edited by R. Villa, J. Thousand, W. Stainback, and S. Stainback. Baltimore: Paul H. Brookes.

Williams, W., T. Fox, J. Thousand, and W. Fox. (1990). "Levels of Acceptance and Implementation of Best Practices in the Education of Students with Severe Handicaps." *Education and Treatment in Mental Retardation* 25, 2: 120–131.

Ysseldyke, J.E. (1987). "Classification of Handicapped Students." In *Handbook of Special Education: Research and Practice, Vol. I: Learner Characteristics and Adaptive Education,* edited by M.C. Wang, M.C. Reynolds, and H.J. Walberg. New York: Pergamon Press.

Voice of Inclusion: My Friend, Ro Vargo

Rosalind and Joe Vargo

> A school should not be a preparation for life. A school should be life.
> —Elbert Hubbard

We often say that we consider our daughter, Ro, a wonderful gift. The people we have met through Ro, the friends we have made, the experiences and lessons in life we have shared and have been taught by living and loving and accepting Ro have been gifts, gifts all. We are not really sure when others began seeing Ro's "giftedness." Likely, it was an evolving process.

Ro has been in inclusive preschool and school-aged educational settings for 12 years now. Each year she has progressed with her peers; she has grown fond of them and they of her.

Kindergarten

Among our vivid kindergarten memories was Ro's first invitation to a birthday party. Kristen's mother phoned to ask if she should make any special arrangements for Ro to attend. Fighting back tears, we responded, "No, but thanks for asking." Kristen's mom said her daughter was so looking forward to Ro coming.

Then we said it. "We love Ro because she's our daughter. But do you know why other kids like her?"

The mom responded, "Well, I can only speak for my daughter, Kristen. She says she likes Ro's smile. She's someone you can really talk to. . . and she wears really neat clothes." She continued, "I think kids like Ro because they can just be themselves around her."

2nd Grade

In 2nd grade Ro had a big birthday party. Since we would be picking up the kids who were invited at school, we needed to know who actually was coming. The night before the party, we called Eric's mom and politely asked, "Is Eric coming to Ro's party tomorrow?"

She said, "I'm sorry I didn't call you, but Eric said he just told Ro in school yesterday that he was coming. Was that all right?"

It was more than all right! To Eric, the fact that Ro didn't talk didn't mean that she didn't understand him.

Shortly thereafter, while attending church on Sunday, we reflected on how feverishly we had worked to get Ro into regular school in order to be exposed to real life learning and living. We began to feel guilty about why we had not persevered in having Ro receive First Holy Communion with her age-mates.

Somewhat apprehensive, we and Ro met one evening with the pastor. Thinking we would have to justify her inclusion, we had all of our appropriate scriptural references and detailed notes to build our case. To our surprise and delight, our pastor agreed wholeheartedly. He said, "You know, we are the ones with hang-ups, not Ro. We are the ones who make all the rules so that people like Ro can't receive Communion." He continued, "I'm excited about Ro receiving our Lord and the effect Ro will have on our parish families' lives when she does."

I mentioned how comfortable we were bringing Ro to church. So many people had already reached out to her.

First Communion day came, and Ro approached the altar. Her dad, Joe, recalls being unable to talk or move until she first received. The liturgy ended with hugs, kisses, and tears. A non-Catholic friend, unaware of the spiritual significance of the day for us, said she was intensely moved seeing Ro in a seemingly transfixed state. This brought back memories of our pastor's words about the potential impact of Ro's Communion on others' lives. We experienced a renewed belief that Christ was in our midst through Ro.

4th Grade

In 4th grade, when kids already were concerned about clothing and hair styles, Ro was voted "Best Friend" by her 25 "typical" 4th grade classmates. Somehow, Ro's inclusion in the school life of many kids was making a tremendous difference; her "giftedness" was recognized and celebrated.

One night that year a puzzling phone call came for Ro. Sharing the same nickname as my daughter, I thought the call was for me. The young girl at the other end of the line clarified, "No, I'd like the Ro who goes to Ed Smith School."

I said, "Hold on," and exclaimed to Joe, "Someone wants to talk with Ro on the phone!" We got Ro up from the dinner table and put the phone to her ear.

Immediately recognizing the voice of her friend, Ghadeer, she started laughing. She then nodded her head to indicate "yes," followed by a head shake indicating "no."

Curiosity got the best of me and I took the phone, reporting to Ghadeer, "Ro's listening and nodding her head."

Ghadeer said, "Great. I asked her advice about a birthday present for a friend. Now, did she nod yes for the jewelry or the board game?"

Ro's 11th Birthday

We remember with pleasure Ro's 11th birthday party. Prior to the party, the mother of one of Ro's friends called to ask if the present she had picked out for Ro was okay. Apparently her daughter hadn't been with her when she picked it out. She had just wrapped it and given it to her daughter to take to school that morning. She wasn't sure if the gift was the "in" thing, fearing her daughter would die of embarrassment if it wasn't.

She had bought Ro a jump rope, a deluxe model. Without hesitation, I said that it was a wonderful idea and a gift that Ro would love using with her sisters. With a sigh of relief, the mom responded, "Well, I'm glad. I was afraid Ro might be handicapped!" For the life of me, I wanted to save this mom obvious embarrassment. But, I said, "Well, she is. . .a little bit." After many of her apologies and my reassurances, we got off the phone as friends. She had made my day, my week, my life! The thought that an 11-year-old girl got a birthday party invitation, wanted to go, and had her mom buy a present—*never thinking it important to mention that her friend had a disability*—still makes me cry with wonderment and happiness.

A later message of acceptance and love came at the birthday party itself when Ro opened the present. All the guests knew that their friend, Ro, had several occupational and physical therapy sessions a week. Yet, when Ro unwrapped the jump rope, every girl was elated, shrieking, "I hope I get one of those for my birthday." and "Oh, cool." They immediately dragged Ro out to the driveway where they tied one end of the jump rope to her wrist. With the strength of her twirling partner, Ro was able to rotate the rope for her friends. It was the best adaptive occupational therapy activity she'd had in months.

A Gift for Ghadeer

A profound testimony to inclusive education occurred in January of 1993. Ghadeer, the friend who had called to ask for advice on a gift selection, suffered a severe stroke. At the age of 12, she was comatose for a month. Teachers prepared classmates, including Ro, for imminent death. However, after weeks of family, teachers, and friends' reading at her bedside, Ghadeer miraculously recovered, but not completely. Her voice and articulation were so impaired that she could not talk. To the amazement of her doctors and nurses, this did not stop her from communicating. She began to use sign language. An interpreter was quickly found, who asked Ghadeer where she had learned sign language. She replied in sign, "From my friend, Ro Vargo!"

After four months of intensive rehabilitative therapy, Ghadeer returned to school, but now as a "special education" student requiring speech and language services, and physical and occupational therapy. Her family proudly reported that Ghadeer turned away the "special" bus and rode the regular school bus on her first day back. Further, she lobbied for a laptop computer to assist her with her schoolwork. Inclusive education enabled Ghadeer to get to know someone like Ro and learn about augmentative communication systems and her rights, particularly her right to be a part of her school, class, and friendship circle. She had learned that a person still belongs even if something unexpected like sustaining a disability happens.

What's Hard About Being Ro's Friend?

Ghadeer was one of many friends who became quite capable of expressing what Ro meant to them and what they learned at school with her. This became clear at a national education conference, when Ro and a group of her friends responded to questions from parents and teachers in a session on building friendships in inclusive classrooms.

Tiffany articulated, "Ro should be in class with all of us. How else is she going to learn the really important stuff? Besides, we learn a lot from her."

When a teacher asked, "Have you ever discussed Ro's disability with her?" Stacey indignantly replied, "No, I know she's different, but I never thought it important to ask. Like, for instance, I never thought to go up to a black kid in my class and say, 'You're black. How come you're different?'"

Another key question was, "What's the hardest thing about being Ro's friend?" As Ro's parents, we held our breath, waiting for responses like, "She drools. She walks funny. She's a messy eater." But again Stacey spoke up, saying, "The hardest thing about being Ro's friend is that she always has a parent or an adult with her." Ouch! That hurt. But it taught us, Ro's parents, an important lesson that surely will positively affect Ro's future.

Transition to Middle School

Ro's transition from elementary to middle school was tough, socially, as it can be for any adolescent. Her first months in middle school were spent in isolation, even though she was in the regular program. The barrier Ro faced was gaining acceptance from her *new* middle school peers. Initially, she was ignored or stared at; a few classmates even teased her. When Ro was assigned to a work group, although no group members verbally complained, they did make nonverbal signs of rejection. In those first months, we began to doubt our decision to include Ro in middle school. We recalled the comment of a teacher the year before who said, "Middle school kids don't like *themselves*. How can you expect them to like *your* kid?"

It was Mauricha, a classmate who became Ro's closest new friend, who broke the social barrier. When asked how they became friends, Mauricha said, "I saw her. She saw me. We've just been friends ever since." By the end of the year, six months after Mauricha broke the ice, things were quite different. Now, when Ro walked down the hall, many acknowledged her with friendly greetings such as, "Hey, Ro! Give me five." If a teacher asked her to quiet down, classmates jumped to her defense with shouts of "Hey, get off her back; don't you know she can't help it?"

One night while I was taking Mauricha home, she looked at me and touched my arm and said, "You know, Mrs. Vargo, lots of teachers think I'm friends with Ro because it gets me more attention. That isn't true. The truth is, I need her more than she needs me. When Ro is down, I can make her smile. But when I'm down, she always makes me smile. It is a kind of a bond."

Mauricha moved on to high school the next year, and on the first day she arrived on our doorstep saying, "Can I come in? I want to tell Ro about my first day." Mauricha came again the following day, this time bringing Joey, too. Under the makeup and "tough guy" appearances were the same honest, open, and sensitive kids we saw in elementary school.

The Future?

Our "severely impaired" child already has accomplished more than we had ever thought possible; and she continues to grow. Also "growing" are Mauricha, Tyrell, Patty, Brandiss, Holly, Quantia, Nicole, Maureen, Joey, and many other young people. They will not seek to discount or harm Ro. Instead, they will be her community. They will be the seekers of social and legislative reform to support the inclusive lifestyle to which Ro and they have grown accustomed. They gladly will be her neighbors, caretakers, job coaches, and friends of tomorrow because they shared *together* in today's classrooms the same space, hopes, and dreams.

4

Managing Complex Change Toward Inclusive Schooling

Jacqueline S. Thousand and Richard A. Villa

We are not alone in struggling with questions about educational reform or the instillation of the ethic and practice of inclusive education in North America. Why is change in some organizations, schools included, so difficult and seemingly unwelcomed, even when overwhelming evidence shows that the status quo is not working for many? Why do expectations for achieving both excellence and equity for all children in our public schools seem, to some, to be beyond reach or ridiculous? Why do people in the midst of change feel confusion, anxiety, resistance, frustration, or that they are on a treadmill, trying to keep up with a plethora of "best practice" initiatives but not having a clear idea of where to start or what direction to take? Why does progress occur in some places and not in others?

Questions like these have nagged us for as long as we have been promoting more inclusive educational options for children with disabilities. Somehow, we *knew* that there *were* understandable ways of leading organizations and people into and through change. But not until we had gone through and observed transformations of school cultures and practices did answers to these questions begin to emerge. This chapter on strategies for organizational change is *not* intended to be one of absolute conclusions or prescriptions, for reasons articulated by Margaret Wheatley in her assumption-shattering *Leadership and the New Science* (1994):

> First, I no longer believe that [school] organizations can be changed by imposing a model developed elsewhere. So little transfers to, or even inspires, those trying to work at change in their own organizations. Second . . . there is no objective reality out there waiting to reveal its secrets. There are no recipes or formulae, no checklists or advice that describe "reality." There is only what we create through our engagement with others and with events. Nothing really transfers; everything is always new and different and unique to each of us (p. 7).

We believe, as does Wheatley, that "we have only just begun the process of discovering and inventing the new organizational forms that will inhabit the twenty-first century" (1994, p. 5); that is, we are only beginning to explore paradigms of schooling that are inclusive and synchronized with the predicted diversity and unpredictability of 21st-century life. We further believe that to be the educational explorers and inventors of tomorrow, we must give up many, if not all, of our ideas of what did and did not work in school just yesterday. Einstein understood all of this long ago, observing that it is impossible to solve the complex problems we face with the same consciousness we had when we created them.

We begin this chapter by examining factors that have made school organizations so intractable in the past. We then examine five variables—vision, skills, incentives, resources, and action planning—that appear to contribute to the successful management of complex change within any organization. The chapter concludes with summary insights into the change process.

Sources of School Intractability

Writing of the school reform efforts of his day, Comenius lamented, "[D]espite all of the effort, [schools] remain exactly the same as they were" (cited in Deal and Peterson 1990, p. 3). Comenius's observation, made more than 350 years ago, has been echoed by many through the centuries, including Sarason in his 1990 work, *The Predictable Failure of School Reform.* What makes schools so intractable? Frequently cited causes are (1) inadequate teacher preparation; (2) inappropriate organizational structures, policies, and procedures; (3) lack of attention to the cultural aspects of schooling; and (4) poor leadership.

Inadequate Teacher Preparation

A first barrier to school change is the categorical approach to teacher preparation in higher education that lacks a curriculum focus on collaborative skills and ethics. In a national survey of teacher preparedness, Lyon, Vaassen, and Toomey (1989) found that 80 percent of teacher respondents indicated they were inadequately prepared through their teacher preparation programs to meet differing student needs. Clearly, colleges and universities share a major responsibility for preparing teachers to both *expect* diversity in the classroom (e.g., the inclusion of children with disabilities in general education) and *develop* the skills to respond to differing student learning styles, rates, and needs. Yet, at a time when teachers are being asked to educate increasingly diverse groups of learners, colleges and universities continue to sort their teacher preparation candidates into categorical programs (e.g., special education, general education, gifted and talented, English as a Second Language) and prepare them to expect to work with only certain types of learners. Sarason (1990) comments on the situation:

> School personnel are graduates of our colleges and universities. It is there that they learn there are at least two types of human beings and if you choose to work with one of them you render yourself legally and conceptually incompetent to work with others (p. 258).

Hawkins (cited in Cobern 1991) described the pervasive and unrecognized role of presuppositions (such as ethics, values, beliefs, and attitudes) and misconceptions of human learners (teachers included) as *deep barriers* to reconceptualizing and to change itself. Some of these deep barriers perpetuated by many teacher preparation programs are identified in the left-hand column of Figure 4.1 and are contrasted with alternative concepts in the right-hand column.

FIGURE 4.1
Deep Barriers and Emerging Concepts in Teacher Preparation

Barrier	Emerging Concept
Tracking and homogeneous grouping are practiced and valued.	Diversity is valued.
Some categories of students do not belong.	All students belong.
Readiness is precursor for entry into learning opportunities.	Learning is an evolutionary and ongoing process that requires no preparation.
Hierarchical relationships exist among professions (e.g., administrators, teachers, paraprofessionals), students, and families.	All adults, students, and members of the community are valued.
Professional preparation maintains existing standards and practice.	Professional preparation imparts the skills to invent and personalize education for every student.
Some proportion of students will fail.	"Failure" implies that the current methodologies did not work and should be changed.

These barriers operate at an unspoken level, guiding everyday actions between teachers and students, teachers and community members, and teacher educators and future educators. These deep barriers unconsciously maintained by many teacher preparation programs prepare graduates to keep the education system as it is, with teachers working alone rather than collaboratively, and students grouped by label (e.g., general education, learning disabled, severely disabled, non-English proficient). Deep barriers blind educators to inventing new methods to meet the needs of individual learners.

Inappropriate Organizational Structures, Policies, and Procedures

"Student diversity is only a problem because of the kind of school organization we have" (Holmes Group 1990).

Inappropriate organizational structures, policies, and procedures often are cited as a second reason for the intractability of schools (Deal 1987). Schools often are compartmentalized organizations that thwart rather than promote collaboration and coordination of resources, ideas, and actions. For example, many schools continue to rely on a lockstep curriculum determined not by the assessment of individual student needs but by the grade level to which students are assigned. Students are placed in a grade according to age and are expected to master a predetermined, arbitrary set of curriculum objectives by the end of each school year. If they fail, they repeat the subject or grade or are referred for special services that pull them out of the general education system for part or all of the day; they become so-called curriculum casualties (Gickling and Thompson 1985).

Additionally, many schools continue to track students into high-, medium-, and low-ability groups, sometimes including pullouts for special services. A formal separation divides general and special education services, with special education being a freestanding "second system" (Wang, Reynolds, and Walberg 1988, p. 248) with its own administration; department; inservice training events; faculty meetings; and policies and procedures for discipline, parent involvement, and access to educational services.

Finally, few schools expect, reward, or otherwise encourage instructional personnel to plan, teach, share professional expertise, or support one another as a team. Little if any time is structured into the work week for such collaboration to occur.

Lack of Attention to Cultural Aspects of Schooling

A third reason suggested for the failure of school reform is resistance to the loss of the familiar tradition or *culture* of school (e.g., "I work alone; my business is none of your business"; "These are my students and those are yours"; "We teach content, and students who can't keep up don't belong"). Culture may be defined as the "historically rooted socially transmitted set of deep patterns of thinking and ways of acting that give meaning to human experiences" (Deal and Peterson 1990, p. 8). The power of culture is that when "attachments to people or objects are [threatened and] broken . . . people experience a deep sense of loss and grief" (Deal 1987, p. 7) comparable to the stages of grief (i.e., denial, resistance, bargaining, acceptance) experienced by someone who has lost a loved one. Thus, when change is on the doorstep, some people (teachers, administrators, and students alike) will feel compelled to dig in their heels and resist, at least initially. Given this, a shift from a fragmented to an inclusive school culture requires change agents to develop new heroes, rituals, traditions, and symbols that celebrate inclusive practices. They might also respond to the inevitable references to the "good old days" with Will Rogers's reminder that "schools aren't as good as they used to be; they never were."

Poor Leadership

A final reason cited in the literature on schools' intractability regarding innovation is that many change agents are naive or cowardly or both (Sarason 1990). They are naive in that they fail to realize or acknowledge just how complex system change is or how long it will take. At a minimum, it takes five to seven years for a change to filter through and become the norm in an organization. Senge (1990) argues that it can take up to 20 years for those who approvingly remember "the way it was" to be gone from the system, so that only those of the "new order" are around to pass on the new culture. Change agents also are naive when they fail to link various change initiatives together (e.g., thematic and interdisciplinary curriculum, multi-aged grouping, inclusive education, multicultural education) or communicate to others how these initiatives support the overall goals of the district, including economic and social self-sufficiency, independent living, full inclusion and integration into society of all students of the community.

Change agents are cowardly when they refuse to deal with the emotional turmoil and conflict that naturally accompany change initiatives or when they leave their positions of leadership before the change they have championed has taken hold. Given that the average tenure of a principal or superintendent in the United States is three years—several years less than the projected time frame for organizational transformation to occur—is it any wonder many educators respond to new educational initiatives with an attitude that says "this is only a fad" or "this too will pass"?

In summary, educational reform occurs when educators *see the big picture,* when they "penetrate the level of immediacy of everyday action and consider the practices of schooling in relation to the social, cultural, political and economic context of education" (Angus 1989, p. 84). For this to happen, those who choose to lead us into change must be aware of the barriers to change and take the risks necessary to overcome them, for "the biggest risk in education is not taking one" (Sarason 1990, p. 176).

Management of Complex Change

We are attracted to Tim Knoster's adaptation (personal communication, December 4, 1991) of Ambrose's (1987) formula for explaining success or failure in managing complex change within an organization. As Figure 4.2 illustrates, at least five variables—vision, skills, incentives, resources, and action planning—factor into a formula for change. If any one variable is left unattended, the result is something other than the desired outcome. The next section of this chapter describes (rather than prescribes) ways to (1) build a vision of inclusive schooling within a community, (2) develop educators' skills and confidence to be inclusive educators, (3) create meaningful incentives for people to risk embarking on an inclusive schooling journey, (4) reorganize and expand human and other resources for teaching to and for diversity, and (5) plan and act on strategies for getting people to see and get excited about a new "big picture."

Building a Vision: Visionizing

"One of the greatest barriers to school reform is the lack of a clear and compelling vision" (Schlechty 1990, p. 137).

Building a vision, or *visionizing,* is the first variable in Knoster's change formula (see Figure 4.2). Unless effort is devoted to building a common vision, confusion for some or many is likely to result.

Visionizing defined. It is widely accepted that "organizations are governed as much by belief and faith as by rationality and outcome" (Deal 1990, p. vi) and that any organizational change initiative is guided by belief and faith in a vision. We use the term *visionizing* (Parnes 1988) to describe the process of creating and communicating a compelling picture of a desired future state and inducing others' commitment to

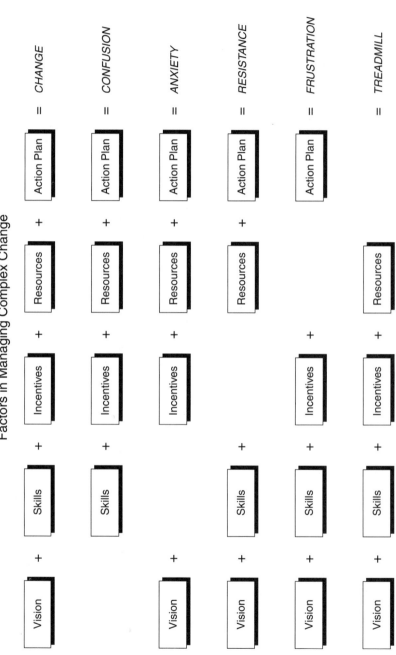

FIGURE 4.2
Factors in Managing Complex Change

Vision		Skills		Incentives		Resources		Action Plan		
Vision	+	Skills	+	Incentives	+	Resources	+	Action Plan	=	CHANGE
		Skills	+	Incentives	+	Resources	+	Action Plan	=	CONFUSION
Vision	+			Incentives	+	Resources	+	Action Plan	=	ANXIETY
Vision	+	Skills	+			Resources	+	Action Plan	=	RESISTANCE
Vision	+	Skills	+	Incentives	+			Action Plan	=	FRUSTRATION
Vision	+	Skills	+	Incentives	+	Resources			=	TREADMILL

that future. We use this term because it suggests the active mental struggle and the "mental journey from the known to the unknown" (Hickman and Silva 1984, p. 151) that people go through when they reconceptualize their beliefs and declare public ownership of a new view.

Leaders in inclusive education stress the importance of clarifying for themselves, school personnel, and the community a vision of success based on assumptions that (1) *all* children are able to learn, (2) *all* children should be educated together in their community's schools, and (3) the school system is responsible for addressing the unique needs of *all* children. To articulate such an inclusive vision is necessary but not sufficient. A community must *adopt* the vision. Visionizing requires fostering widespread understanding and consensus regarding the vision.

Consensus building through an examination of rationales for change. One strategy for building consensus is to share with others the theoretical, ethical, and databased rationales for inclusive education that address their personal concerns. Norm Kunc (personal communication, June 25, 1994) suggests conceptualizing each person as a circle with two halves, one half representing the person's *concerns* and the other half the person's *beliefs* (supportive or nonsupportive) about a proposition such as inclusive education. Kunc argues that to shift a person's belief in favor of a proposition, we must first identify the person's concerns (questions, fears, nightmares, confusions) regarding the proposition. Stated otherwise, as change agents we must solicit and listen to the concerns of everyone likely to be affected by inclusive schooling. That is why in the previous chapter we asked you to identify the rationales for change most compelling (i.e., most likely to bring up priority concerns) for you and the other stakeholders in your community. Fiscal and legal rationales may speak to the concerns of administrators and school board members; disappointing efficacy data may speak to parents of students with and without disabilities and to the students themselves; procedural issues and the disjointed and incremental nature of special service systems may speak to special educators tired of isolation and endless hours of paperwork.

Once concerns are revealed, opportunities can be structured to communicate supporting information for each rationale. This information may address concerns and positively alter beliefs. It may be communicated in any number of ways—through inservice training events, distribution of readings with follow-up discussions, one-on-one dialogues, community forums, videotapes of and visitations to schools that have adopted inclusive visions and successfully transformed, and so on. Knowledge of concerns also helps in the move from visionizing to action planning in that it prompts us to regularly and vigilantly ask, "How can we assure that people's worst nightmares (concerns) do not come true?"

Visionizing allows us to replace an old culture with a new one and simultaneously manage the personal loss that cultural change inevitably stirs in the people affected. New histories, heroes, and rituals must be constructed; and that occurs when traditional solutions (e.g., adding a new program) and other educational inequities (e.g., the discrimination that may accompany tracking, special education, and gifted and talented programs) are publicly identified as being ineffective, inefficient, and counter to the desired vision (i.e., inclusive learning opportunities). New language and labels that are *educative* (Schlechty 1990) rather than *deficit oriented* must be introduced, and people must be expected to use them. For example, if children are to be valued for their differences, it is more educative to refer to children in "person first" language (e.g., "Cecilia, who has Down syndrome"; "Juan, who is not yet English proficient") rather than deficit-oriented language (e.g., "the Down syndrome kids"; "the LEPs—Limited English Proficient").

Consensus building through mission statements. A second powerful strategy for securing support for an inclusive vision is to involve representatives of school and community stakeholder groups in examining the current district or school mission statement and reformulating a mission and objectives for supporting all students. Engaging people in such participatory decision making results in greater "ownership" of the resultant statement than if it were imposed on them (Thousand and Villa 1992). Although probably an obvious and unnecessary caution, we urge that separate mission statements never be formulated for special versus general education, as this simply perpetuates "dual system" thinking and action.

Clearly, risks are involved in turning over such an important function to a group of people who, based on their diverse professional and personal perspectives, initially will differ in the degree of their support for inclusive education. This risk, however, can be minimized by ensuring that the committee has been informed of the ethical, theoretical, and databased rationales for inclusive education (as offered in Chapter 3) and that the committee includes at least some members who have an in-depth understanding of and commitment to inclusive education. While the clarification and promotion of an inclusive school philosophy in the form of a mission statement is an important symbolic and guiding endeavor, it is important to recognize that a school community need not have a formal statement to alter organizational structures and instructional approaches that bar the inclusion of all students.

Consensus building by respecting what we expect. Consensus for inclusive education can be fostered by respecting what we expect: that is, encouraging, recognizing, and publicly acknowledging staff and students who plunge in as early innovators and pioneers, and model and actively promote the philosophy of inclusion. In structuring recognition, staff and students should be asked what they consider rewarding (e.g., for some, public recognition would be embarrassing, but an opportunity to attend a conference might be a treat). Further, any person— secretary, cafeteria worker, volunteer—should be a candidate for acknowledgment, since every person has the power through word or action to advance or impede a vision.

Who should be a visionizer? Who can or should initiate change? We suggest that anyone can be a visionizer or change agent. "It's not important where on the organizational chart the person falls; what is important is that facilitators support, help, assist, and nurture" (Hord, Rutherford, Huling-Austin, and Hall 1987, p. 3). Visionizers understand that change means cultural transformation, which can take many years; they stick around for the long haul and do not leave when times get tough.

Visionizers know their job is to create cognitive dissonance, discomfort, chaos, and a sense of urgency, perhaps even rage, in the school and community. This type of leadership by passion works to initiate change because, as others observe and feel the outrage, their own emotional potential is kindled within themselves. "Outrage tells people what is important" (Sergiovanni 1992, p. 74). So visionizers "talk up" the vision and supporting innovations and innovators, persuade people to adopt the vision, and coach them to perform their daily work in accordance with the vision. Although they take every opportunity to build consensus, they know that no single "teaching strategy" or "learning style" is privileged; strategies will vary by community, reflecting that community's unique demographics, history, and current beliefs. Finally, visionizers know that change is a very personal process and that the best way to get people to risk the unfamiliar is to listen to their concerns, believe in them, and give them the opportunities, training, and support to try.

Skill Building to Educate in an Inclusive School

In Knoster's change formula (see Figure 4.2), a school system can have vision, incentives, resources, and an action plan, but unless educators believe they have the *skills* to respond to the needs of students and others, the outcome likely will be *anxiety* rather than success due to educators' doubts about their ability to be "good teachers." Clearly, the more diverse the student body, the more skilled educators must be as a *collective* instructional body. We highlight the word *collective* to emphasize that members of a school faculty need not have the same content and instructional skills; they do, however, need to be able to readily access one another so they can share their skills across students and classrooms.

No matter how exciting or promising an innovation, to clarify its nuances educators need training, guided practice and feedback, and opportunities to solve problems with colleagues (Joyce and Showers 1988). Further, for the innovation to become the "new culture," people must come to understand how the innovation is significant to their personal and professional growth and the growth of their students (Hord et al. 1987). Within the context of inclusive education, this places training front and center as a strategy for reducing anxiety and transforming the culture of the school.

Areas of common training. A large proportion of teachers report that neither their professional preparation nor their relatively isolated teaching experiences have adequately prepared them for the inclusive education paradigm (Lyon et al. 1989). Thus, it becomes a local school district's responsibility to craft and gain ratification of an ongoing comprehensive inservice training agenda that research and theory suggest will develop "innovation-related knowledge, performance skills, and positive attitudes" (Hord et al. 1987, p. 76) and increase the number of people who can perform desired new behaviors successfully.

Teachers need to acquire core skills, such as those described in Chapter 5 and supplemented in Chapter 8, to be responsive to likely student needs. Whatever the content selected for a school's capacity-building inservice training agenda, it must be vision driven. An example, shown in Figure 4.3, is the four-tiered, four-year inservice agenda for implementing the "heterogeneous schooling" vision of Winooski,

FIGURE 4.3
Winooski, Vermont, Public School Inservice Training Agenda
for Heterogeneous (Inclusive) Schooling

Level I **Generic Content Relevant for All Members of the School and Greater Community**
- Rationales for heterogeneous schooling (inclusive education)
- General education research regarding the characteristics of "effective" schools and current exemplary "best practices" from general and special education
- Models for adult collaboration and teaming and the development of small-group social skills

Level II **Selected Content to Respond to Self-Identified Training Needs of Parents and Community Members**
- Legal rights and procedural safeguards
- Individual Education Plans (IEPs)
- Discipline systems that teach responsibility
- Community-referenced instruction and assessment
- Transition between school environments
- Future planning for and transition to post-school supports
- Post-high school follow-up

Level III **Training in Assessment, Discipline, and Instructional Strategies for Instructional Personnel**
- Outcome-based instructional models
- Family-centered and curriculum-based assessment models
- Curriculum adaptation approaches
- Peer-mediated instructional strategies (e.g., cooperative group learning, peer tutoring)
- Classroom and schoolwide behavior management and discipline approaches
- Methods for teaching and reinforcing students' use of positive social skills

Level IV **Training in Peer Coaching and Clinical Supervision for Faculty and Supervisory Personnel**

Vermont (Villa 1989, Villa and Thousand 1992a). It is important to empower and motivate staff in their learning by letting them choose how they receive training (e.g., courses, mentoring, team teaching, summer institutes, workshop series).

Who receives training? As Figure 4.3 suggests, everyone is a candidate for inservice training because anyone can resist or support inclusive education. Although initial training may be organized for and delivered to innovators and early adopters in the school, eventually *everyone* involved—teachers, administrators, paraeducators, related service personnel, secretarial and support staff, students, school board members, parents, other community members—needs to acquire a common core of knowledge like that identified in Tier I of Figure 4.3. No one *directly* involved in the change can be exempt from participation in training for skill building (Tier III of Figure 4.3) if sustainable, widespread change is to occur. To excuse those who are reluctant, resistant, or apathetic from acquiring the disposition and skills to implement inclusive educational practices divides people, promotes the development of factions, fosters resentment toward the nonparticipants, reinforces a "this too will pass" mentality, and generally works against the development of a unified new culture.

Training in support of inclusive education never ends. New staff must be inducted into the values and practices of the system. People need continual renewal through training that allows them to impart their skills to others and refine further what they already do well.

Incentives to Engage People in Inclusive Schooling

Returning to Knoster's change formula (Figure 4.2), a school system can have a vision; personnel can have skills and abundant resources; a plan of action can be set into motion; yet, without incentives that are meaningful to each individual affected by the change, the outcome may be passive or active resistance rather than excited engagement.

Although incentives are important ingredients in a change formula, heavy reliance on *extrinsic* incentives (e.g., honors, financial awards) can interfere with change, as Sergiovanni (1990) explains:

> Traditional management theory is based on the principle "what gets rewarded gets done." . . . [Unfortunately,] when rewards can no longer be provided the work no longer will be done. Work performance becomes contingent upon a barter-

ing arrangement rather than being self-sustaining because of moral principle or a deeper psychological connection. A better strategy upon which to base our efforts is "what is rewarding gets done." When something is rewarding it gets done even when "no one is looking" (p. 22).

We promote more *intrinsic* incentives that move people to action

> because of obligations, duties, a sense of righteousness, felt commitments, and other reasons with moral overtones . . . [or because of] finding what they are doing to be personally significant in its own right (Sergiovanni 1992, p. 58).

Intrinsic motivators include recognition of one's own increased effectiveness as evidenced by student development and happiness, pride in one's own professional risk taking and growth and accompanying recognition from respected colleagues and students, feelings of personal satisfaction, and the experience of *flow*—

> the state in which people are so involved in an activity that nothing else seems to matter; the experience itself is so enjoyable that people will do it even at great cost, for the sheer sake of doing it (Csikszentmihalyi 1990, p. 4).

Genuine and sustainable changes in culture and dedication to inclusive schooling depend on people who come to be motivated more by their emotions, values, beliefs, and social bonds with colleagues than by outside forces.

Capitalizing on social bonds through the development of an *esprit de corps*—a common spirit of inspiring enthusiasm, devotion, and intense regard for the vision and honor of the group—can be a powerful incentive for change. To promote esprit de corps, regard teams as well as individuals; highlight the importance of and pride in collaborative efforts. Second, spend time "in the trenches" with teachers and students, learning what they are doing well that can be publicly and privately acknowledged. Third, ask staff and students what *they* value as an incentive (e.g., notes of praise, travel to conferences or other schools engaged in inclusive education, opportunities to make presentations, fine tuning innovations). What is rewarding to one person may be of little significance to another. Finally, overlook no one; a bus driver or custodian can do as much to hasten the acceptance or demise of inclusive education as can an administrator or professional educator.

Resources for Inclusive Education

Continuing with Knoster's change formula (Figure 4.2), if people in a school system feel they lack the needed resources to do the job, they likely will experience frustration that can zap their energy and enthusiasm and draw them away from their change efforts. Resources in education may be *technical* and *material* (e.g., paper and pencils, computer hardware and software, curriculum materials and concepts) or *organizational* (i.e., how the day, week, year, and people within the school are organized). Time is an important organizational resource that is "not *auxiliary* to teaching responsibilities—nor is it 'released time' from them. It is absolutely central to such responsibilities, and essential to making school succeed" (Raywid 1993, p. 34). Yet many schools suffer from a great shortage of time. Figure 4.4 shows how some schools have attempted to meet the time challenge. (See Raywid 1993 for expanded and additional examples.)

Clearly, educators' perceptions of the adequacy of the technical, material, and organizational resources available to them influence their work satisfaction. Nevertheless, the *human* resource—relationships with other adults and children and their unique gifts, talents, and trades—is arguably the most important for school health and improvement. Support from colleagues, students, formal leadership, and others in the community is what most people really are crying out for when they scream they are frustrated and in need of resources. Currently, much discussion centers around teacher and student empowerment, inviting all members of the school community to make decisions about things that affect them. Empowerment may be an important resource (and incentive) for change; but interdependence with and support from others is as essential, as Sergiovanni (1992) points out:

> A virtuous school gives as much attention to enablement as it does to empowerment; it considers the two to be interdependent parts of the same whole: People should have both the discretion and whatever assistance they need to use it wisely (p. 117).

Structuring access to adult resources through role redefinition. Teaching has been characterized as a "lonely profession" (Sarason, Levine, Godenberg, Cherlin, and Bennet 1966, p. 74). Teachers get the message that "I am in this pretty much alone, alone with my students

FIGURE 4.4
Strategies for Expanding Time for Collaborative Planning, Teaching, and Reflection

- Ask staff to identify with whom and when they need to collaborate and redesign the master schedule to accommodate these needs.
- Hire "permanent substitutes" to rotate through classrooms to periodically "free up" teachers to attend meetings during the day rather than before or after school.
- Institute a community service component to the curriculum; when students are in the community (e.g., Thursday afternoon) teachers meet.
- Schedule "specials" (e.g., art, music), clubs, and tutorials during the same time blocks (e.g. first and second period), so teachers have one or two hours a day to collaborate.
- Engage parents and community members to plan and conduct half-day or full-day exploratory, craft, hobby (e.g., gourmet cooking, puppetry, photography), theater, or other experiential programs.
- Partner with colleges and universities; have their faculty teach in the school or offer TV lessons, demonstrations, on-campus experiences to free up school personnel.
- Rearrange the school day to include a 50- to 60-minute block of time before or after school for collaborative meeting and planning.
- Lengthen the school day for students by 15 to 30 minutes per day. The cumulative "extra" student contact hours each month allow for periodic early dismissal of students and time for teachers to meet.
- Earmark some staff development days for collaborative meetings.
- Use faculty meeting time for small-group meetings to solve problems related to issues of immediate and long-range importance.
- Build into the school schedule at least one "collaboration day" per marking period or month.
- Lengthen the school year for staff but not for students, or shorten the school year for students but not staff.
- Go to year-round schooling with three-week breaks every quarter; devote four or five of the three-week intersession days to teacher collaboration.

behind this door" from various sources: (1) the organization of schools into separate classrooms of *one* teacher for so many students, (2) job descriptions and teacher evaluation procedures that emphasize individual rather than collaborative performance, and (3) teacher preparation programs (e.g., "solo" versus "collaborative" teaching as the culminating practicum event, and distinct "regular" versus "special" education training programs). The silliness of teaching in isolation is obvious. Yet the norms, traditions, and organization of many schools perpetuate segregation of staff and students, as well as inflexible, standard expectations as to the role of people with different labels (e.g., "administrator," "teacher," "paraeducator," "specialist," "parent").

We propose that for educators to most readily access the resources of other educational personnel, everyone in the school system must stop thinking and acting in standard, isolated ways. Everyone must relinquish traditional roles, drop distinct professional labels, and redistribute their job functions across any number of other people (Cross and Villa 1992, Thousand and Villa 1990, Thousand and Villa 1992). Figure 4.5 shows how job functions can and have changed in schools that meld human resources through dramatic, systemwide role redefinition. It must be emphasized that flexibility and fluidity is the main aim of role redefinition. Exactly who does what from one year to the next should always be up in the air and determined by the needs of students and the complementary skills (and needs) of the educators involved.

Job titles and formal definitions do influence how people behave. Thus, to further signal and symbolize a change in culture, new policies and job descriptions should be formulated to expect, inspect, and respect a collaborative ethic. In Vermont, a number of school districts have achieved this by creating a single job description for all professional educators (e.g., classroom teachers, special educators, school nurse, guidance personnel) that identifies collaboration and shared responsibility for educating all of a community's children as expected job functions (see a sample job description in Cross and Villa 1992).

Merging resources through teaching team arrangements. Shifting job functions and making them more fluid provide the opportunity to rearrange school personnel in a variety of collaborative relationships—mentoring and peer coaching teams, peer systems that pair newly hired teachers with veterans, and *teaching teams*—

> an organizational and instructional arrangement of two or more members of the school and greater community who distribute among themselves planning, instructional, and evaluation responsibilities for the same students on a regular basis for an extended period of time (Thousand and Villa 1990, p. 152).

FIGURE 4.5
Changes in Job Responsibilities of School Personnel
Before and After Role Redefinition

Job Title	Traditional Responsibilities	Redefined Responsibilities
General Education Administrator	Manages the general education program. Cedes responsibility for special programs to special education administrators, although special programs are "housed" within general education facilities.	Manages the educational programs for *all* students. Articulates the vision and provides emotional support to staff as they experience the change process. Participates as a member of collaborative problem-solving teams that invent solutions to barriers inhibiting the successful inclusion and education of any child. Secures resources to enable staff to meet the needs of all children.
Teacher	Refers students who do not "fit" into the traditional program for diagnosis, remediation, and possible removal. Teaches children who "fit" within the standard curriculum.	Shares responsibility with special educators and other support personnel for teaching all assigned children. Seeks support of special educators and other support personnel for students experiencing difficulty in learning. Collaboratively plans and teaches with other members of the staff and community to meet the needs of all learners.

(continued on next page)

FIGURE 4.5—*Continued*

Job Title	Traditional Responsibilities	Redefined Responsibilities
Teacher *(continued)*		Recruits and trains students to be tutors and social supports for one another.
Special Educator	Provides instruction to students eligible for services in resource rooms, special classes, and special schools.	Collaborates with general educators and other support personnel to meet the needs of all learners. Team teaches with regular educators in general education classes. Recruits and trains students to be peer tutors and social supports for one another.
Psychologist	Tests, diagnoses, assigns labels, and determines eligibility for students' admissionto special programs.	Collaborates with teachers to define problems. Creatively designs interventions. Team teaches. Provides social skills training to classes of students. Conducts authentic assessments. Trains students to be conflict mediators, peer tutors, and supports for one another. Offers counseling to students.

FIGURE 4.5—*Continued*

Job Title	Traditional Responsibilities	Redefined Responsibilities
Support Staff (e.g., social worker, speech and language pathologist, physical therapist)	Diagnoses, labels, and provides direct services to students in settings other than the classroom. Provides support only to students eligible for a particular special program.	Assesses and provides direct services to students within general education classrooms and community settings. Supports students not eligible for special education. Trains classroom teachers, instructional assistants, volunteers, and students to carry out support services. Shares responsibility to meet the needs of all students.
Paraeducator (Teaching assistant)	Works in segregated programs. If working in general education classrooms, stays in close proximity to and works only with student(s) eligible for special services.	Provides services to a variety of students in general education settings. Facilitates natural peer supports within general education settings.
Student	Primarily works independently and competes with other students for "best" performance. Acts as a passive recipient of learning.	Often works with other students in cooperative learning arrangements. Is actively involved in instruction, advocacy, and decision making for self and others.

Members of teaching teams bring their unique instructional expertise, areas of curriculum background, and personal interests together to provide a richer learning experience for all students. Other results are a higher teacher/student ratio, enhanced problem-solving capacity, and more immediate and accurate diagnosis of student needs and delivery of appropriate instruction (Thousand and Villa 1992).

Administrator's role as a resource. School administrators are a critical resource to educators in a number of ways. For example, they can work with teachers and the community to create meaningful incentives and more time for adult, face-to-face interaction. Administrators are a vital source of teacher *support,* as Littrel, Billingsley, and Cross (1994) discovered in their examination of the effects of principal support on special and general educators' stress, job satisfaction, school commitment, health, and intent to stay in teaching. They found that administrators offer different types of support (e.g., *instrumental*—helping teachers with their work; *appraisal*—offering feedback or clarifying job responsibilities; *informational*—providing information and resources). Yet, the type of support principals offer is not always the type educators consider most important. Specifically, *emotional* support—showing teachers they are esteemed and worthy of concern through "open communication, showing appreciation, taking an interest in teachers' work, and considering teachers' ideas" (Littrel et al. 1994, p. 297)— emerged as the most important type of support for administrators to provide.

Students as untapped resources. The terms *teaming* and *collaboration* usually conjure up images of adults joining forces. Schools attempting inclusive education, however, have discovered the importance of practicing what they preach regarding collaboration by sharing their instructional and decision-making power with students in a climate of mutual respect (Villa and Thousand, 1992b). Among the limitless possibilities of collaborative arrangements that could and have benefited students and educators alike are: (1) students as instructors in partner learning, cooperative group learning, and adult-student teaching team arrangements (see Chapter 5 for further explanation); (2) students sitting on their own and classmates' IEP planning teams to advocate for their own or a friend's interests; and (3) students sharing decision-making responsibility by serving on school or district committees, such as curriculum and discipline committees and the school board.

Outside partnerships for change. A school district can gain much needed human, political, and fiscal resources by developing partnerships with state department of education personnel, faculty of higher education institutions, and other school districts with a similar interest in inclusive education. State personnel may provide fiscal incentives or regulatory relief for innovations. They may provide valuable public relations support, articulating the need for inclusive schooling in circulars, publications, and public presentations.

Higher education–school district collaboration offers mutual benefits. Together, the two organizations can design and solicit state or federal support for model demonstrations; arrange for valuable internship experiences for students in teacher preparation programs; conduct research to document the challenges, solutions, and impact of inclusive schooling practices; or codevelop and deliver coursework related to new roles or skills necessary for inclusive educational practice. Finally, schools with a common vision of inclusive education can multiply resources by jointly working to overcome barriers to change, forming coalitions to advocate for change in outdated teacher preparation programs and state-level funding formulas and policies, celebrating successes together, and sharing or exchanging human resources (e.g., reciprocal inservice presenters, joint hiring of a specialist in nonverbal communication).

Planning and Taking Action

Action planning is the last of the five variables in Knoster's change formula (see Figure 4.2). Individuals within a system may have everything else, but without widespread coordinated planning for action, attempting change may be like running on a treadmill. People expend lots of energy but end up in a place not much different from where they were before. Action planning means being thoughtful and communicative about the *process* of change—how, with whom, and in what sequence the steps or stages of change are formulated, communicated, and set into motion. Action plans are tricky, for they require the right mix of planning versus action and the continual involvement of those affected by the change.

Benefits of involvement and communication in planning. Engaging people in action planning for a change that will affect them is essential. Participatory planning encourages individuals' ownership for the coming changes, and it helps people to prepare for change by getting them to believe that change really *will* occur. Planning is the alarm signaling to everyone that things no longer will be the same.

Cautions concerning "overplanning." Alex Osborn (1953), a pioneer in the field of creativity, was noted for his observation that a fair idea put into action was much better than a good idea left on the polishing wheel. He recognized that it is possible to literally plan something to death; unless planning quickly leads to action, interest will wane. Schlechty (1990) acknowledged the same when suggesting that we take a "ready, fire, aim" (rather than "ready, aim, fire") approach to planning change initiatives. Abstract planning divorced from action becomes a cerebral activity of conjuring up a world that does not exist (Wheatley 1994, p. 37).

Successful visionizers and facilitators of school change understand the organic nature of schools; that is, adjustments in even the smallest part affect other parts in ways that almost assuredly are unpredictable. People involved in a change process such as the transition to inclusive schooling, then, must become comfortable with the unknown and "go with the flow." They must accept that notions of how long change will take, the exact steps to be taken along the way, and precisely how things will finally look must be adjusted and readjusted throughout the change process.

Principles of "somewhat" systematic planning. Having stated the caveats regarding overplanning and flexibility, we urge school districts initiating inclusive education not to make the mistake that some have in not having any planning *process*. Action plans for change can take many forms and may use various decision-making processes. Whatever approach a district adopts must lead to regular, observable action. Guiding principles for planning include the following:

• *Look outside.* Throughout the change process, gather and pay close attention to information about social, political, cultural, and economic trends outside the world of school. This can be critical to adoption by the community at large.

• *Look inside, too.* The school system already has resources and strengths as well as barriers to successful education. Carefully examine and discover the current internal strengths and weaknesses of the school system's policies, practices, organizational structures, and so forth.

• *Include stakeholders.* Be sure all relevant stakeholder groups are represented in planning processes and decision making and are communicated with regularly. People are at the core of change; we cause or impede it.

• *Monitor the change.* Change is dynamic—the forces that drive and restrain change shift over time, and the outcome of actions taken is unpredictable. Therefore, it is crucial to meet regularly to review progress, revise and modify plans, disband subgroups that have accomplished their tasks, and create new ad hoc teams to develop action plans for additional needed strategies.

• *Revisit the vision.* The vision can get lost or distorted over time. New people entering the school system and the community may be unaware of or misunderstand the vision. Thus, it is important to keep people on track by periodically reexamining the vision and using the media (e.g., school newsletters, TV spots, newspaper articles) to educate the public.

• *Put things in writing.* People do best if their decisions are put into a written format (an action plan) that specifies in some detail who will do what, by when, and according to what criteria.

Evaluation of action planning. An integral part of action planning is regular and continuous evaluation. What is worth evaluating? Clearly, in the case of inclusion, we want to know if educating children with disabilities in general education is "working." Are students with and without disabilities experiencing elements of the "Circle of Courage" (Brendtro, Brokenleg, and Van Bockern 1990)—belonging, mastery, independence, and generosity—and academic success? What are the postschool outcomes (e.g., employment, continuing education, civic contributions)? What about affective and process variables, such as educators' feelings at various points during the change process and their *stages of concern* (e.g., from little involvement, to informational and personal concerns, to refinement and management concerns) (Hall and Hord 1987). Both outcome and affective/process evaluations offer change agents information needed to adjust the action plan and deal with emerging concerns, failures, confusions, and successes.

Any question important enough for a stakeholder to pose is worth answering (evaluating); that is, whatever is important to someone should be a possible item for evaluation. The evaluation agenda should also be as flexible and open as the planning process. Sometimes quite unexpected outcomes occur. For example, a teenager we know who had been educated in segregated classes in her elementary years experienced a 25-point increase in her tested IQ after two years of full inclusion in her local high school (J. Pauley, personal communication, December 1, 1994). The lesson is that everyone needs to keep an eye out for the unexpected and act as action researchers who note and talk about what they experience in school day to day.

Assumptions in developing action plans. Senge (1990) emphasizes that in healthy organizations, people self-examine their unconscious assumptions about how the organization operates. People involved in a healthy systems change effort must do likewise. They further are advised to adopt some healthy assumptions regarding action planning: (1) no amount of knowledge ever clarifies which action is the "correct" one to take; (2) my own version of the change or the action plan is not necessarily the one that will or should result; (3) manageability is achieved by thinking big and starting small; (4) lack of participation or commitment is not necessarily a rejection of the vision; other factors (e.g., insufficient skills, incentives, or resources) may be the cause; (5) changing culture, not installing an innovation, is the real agenda; (6) any action plan must be based on at least the above assumptions (Fullan and Stiegelbauer 1991).

❦   ❦   ❦

"The difficult we do immediately; the impossible takes a little longer" (Anonymous).

We currently know certain things about the change process in schools. We know, for example, that schools are cultures and that to implement a new vision of schooling, a new culture must replace the old. We know that change inevitably creates cognitive and interpersonal conflict that can be managed through perspective taking and creative problem solving (Parnes 1988). We know that for fundamental change to occur, the roles, rules, relationships, and responsibilities of everyone (students included) will be redefined; hierarchical power relationships have to be altered so everyone affected by impending change has a voice and role in decision making. We know that change is not necessarily progress; only close attention to valued outcomes will tell us if change equals progress. We know that action planning is important and that resources, incentives, and skill building make a difference. We know that commitment to a change often does not occur until people have developed skills and gained experience with the change (McLaughlin 1991) and that initial negative or neutral feelings toward inclusion can and do change (Thousand, Villa, Meyers, and Nevin 1994).

Clearly, the monumental and complex nature of reengineering schooling can become overwhelming. Yet, an increasing number of communities are making the choice to implement with integrity and quality a vision of inclusive education (e.g., see Association for Supervision and Curriculum Development 1994; Villa, Thousand, Stainback, and Stainback 1992). *Choice* is a key word here, as Senge (1990) points out. *Choice* is different than *desire*. Try an experiment. Say, "I want." Now say, "I choose." What is the difference? For most people, "I want" is passive; "I choose" is active. For most, wanting is a state of deficiency— we want what we do not have. Choosing is a state of sufficiency—electing to have what we truly want. For most of us, as we look back over our life, we can see that certain choices we made played a pivotal role in how our life developed. So, too, will the choices we make in the future (p. 360).

Effective inclusive school organizations can be crafted. They are crafted by individuals—individuals who choose to be courageous and engage what we know about change processes to steward a larger vision.

References

Ambrose, D. (1987). *Managing Complex Change.* Pittsburgh, Pa.: The Enterprise Group, Ltd.

Angus, L. (1989). "New Leadership and the Possibilities of Educational Reform." In *Critical Perspectives on Educational Leadership,* edited by J. Smyth. New York: The Falmer Press.

Association for Supervision and Curriculum Development. (1994). *Educational Leadership: The Inclusive School* 52, 4.

Brendtro, L., M. Brokenleg, and S. Van Bockern. (1990). *Reclaiming Youth at Risk: Our Hope for the Future.* Bloomington, Ind.: National Education Service.

Cobern W. (1991). *World View Theory and Science Education Research.* Monograph No. 3. National Association for Research in Science Teaching. Cincinnati, Ohio: University of Cincinnati.

Cross, G., and R. Villa. (1992). "The Winooski School System: An Evolutionary Perspective of a School Restructuring for Diversity." In *Restructuring for Caring and Effective Education: An Administrative Guide to Creating Heteroge-*

neous Schools, edited by R. Villa, J. Thousand, W. Stainback, and S. Stainback. Baltimore: Paul H. Brookes.

Csikszentmihalyi, M. (1990). *Flow: The Psychology of Optimal Experience.* New York: Harper Collins.

Deal, T. (1987). "The Culture of Schools." In *Leadership: Examining the Elusive,* edited by L. Shieve and M. Schoenheit. Alexandria, Va.: Association for Supervision and Curriculum Development.

Deal, T. (1990). Foreword. In *Value-added Leadership: How to Get Extraordinary Performance in Schools,* edited by T.J. Sergiovanni. San Diego: Harcourt Brace Jovanovich.

Deal, T., and K. Peterson. (1990). *The Principal's Role in Shaping School Culture.* Washington D.C.: U.S. Government Printing Office.

Fullan, M.G., and S. Stiegelbauer. (1991). *The New Meaning of Educational Change.* 2nd ed. New York: Teachers College Press.

Gickling, E.E., and V.P. Thompson. "A Personal View of Curriculum-based Assessment." *Exceptional Children* 52: 205–218.

Hall, G.E., and S. Hord. (1987). *Change in Schools: Facilitating the Process.* Albany: State University of New York Press.

Hickman, C., and M. Silva. (1984). *Creating Excellence: Managing Corporate Culture, Strategy, and Change in the New Age.* New York: New American Library.

The Holmes Group. (1990). *Tomorrow's Schools: Principles for the Design of Professional Development Schools.* East Lansing, Mich.: Author.

Hord, S., W. Rutherford, L. Huling-Austin, and G. Hall. (1987). *Taking Charge of Change.* Alexandria, Va.: Association for Supervision and Curriculum Development.

Joyce, B., and B. Showers. (1988). *Student Achievement Through Staff Development.* New York: Longman Publishing Co.

Knoster, T. Personal communication, December 4, 1991.

Kunc, N. Personal communication, June 25, 1994.

Littrell, P.C., B.S. Billingsley, and L.H. Cross. (1994). "The Effects of Principal Support on Special and General Educators' Stress, Job Satisfaction, School Commitment, Health, and Intent to Stay in Teaching." *Remedial and Special Education* 15, 5: 297–310.

Lyon, G.R., M. Vaassen, and F. Toomey. (1989). "Teachers' Perceptions of Their Undergraduate and Graduate Preparation." *Teacher Education and Special Education* 12, 4: 164–169.

McLaughlin, M.V. (1991). In *Education Policy Implementation,* edited by A.R. Oden. Albany: State University of New York Press.

Osborn, A. (1953). *Applied Imagination: Principles and Procedures of Creative Thinking.* New York: Charles Scribner's Sons.

Parnes, S.J. (1988). *Visionizing: State-of-the-Art Processes for Encouraging Innovative Excellence.* East Aurora, N.Y.: D.O.K. Publishers.

Pauley, J. Personal communication, December 1, 1994.

Raywid, M.A. (1993). "Finding Time for Collaboration." *Educational Leadership* 51, 1: 30–34.

Sarason, S., M. Levine, I. Godenberg, D. Cherlin, and E. Bennet (1966). *Psychology in Community Settings: Clinical, Educational, Vocational and Social Aspects.* New York: John Wiley & Sons.

Sarason, S. (1990). *The Predictable Failure of School Reform: Can We Change Course Before It's Too Late?* San Francisco: Jossey-Bass.

Schlechty, P. (1990). *Schools for the 21st Century: Leadership Imperatives for Educational Reform.* San Francisco: Jossey-Bass Publishers.

Senge, P. (1990). *The Fifth Discipline: The Art and Practice of the Learning Organization.* New York: Doubleday.

Sergiovanni, T.J. (1990). *Value-added Leadership: How to Get Extraordinary Performance in Schools.* Orlando, Fla.: Harcourt Brace Jovanovich.

Sergiovanni, T.J. (1992). *Moral Leadership: Getting to the Heart of School Improvement.* San Francisco: Jossey-Bass.

Thousand, J., and R. Villa. (1990). "Sharing Expertise and Responsibilities Through Teaching Teams." In *Support Networks for Inclusive Schooling: Interdependent Integrated Education,* edited by W. Stainback and S. Stainback. Baltimore: Paul H. Brookes.

Thousand, J., and R. Villa. (1992). "Collaborative Teams: A Powerful Tool in School Restructuring." In *Restructuring for Caring and Effective Education: An Administrative Guide for Creating Heterogeneous Schools,* edited by R. Villa, J. Thousand, W. Stainback, and S. Stainback. Baltimore: Paul H. Brookes.

Thousand, J., R. Villa, H. Meyers, and A. Nevin. (April 1994). "The Heterogeneous Education Teacher Survey: A Retrospective Analysis of Heterogeneous (Full Inclusion) Education." Paper presented at the annual meeting of the American Educational Research Association, New Orleans.

Villa, R. (1989). "Model Public School Inservice Programs: Do They Exist?" *Teacher Education and Special Education* 12, 4: 173–176.

Villa, R., and J. Thousand. (1992a). "How One District Integrated Special and General Education." *Educational Leadership* 50, 2: 39–41.

Villa, R., and J. Thousand. (1992b). "Student Collaboration: An Essential for Curriculum Delivery in the 21st Century." In *Curriculum Considerations in Inclusive Classrooms: Facilitating Learning for All Students,* edited by S. Stainback and W. Stainback. Baltimore: Paul H. Brookes.

Villa, R., J. Thousand, W. Stainback, and S. Stainback. (1992). *Restructuring for Caring and Effective Education: An Administrative Guide to Creating Heterogeneous Schools.* Baltimore: Paul H. Brookes.

Wang, M.C., M.C. Reynolds, and H.J. Walberg. (1988). "Integrating Children of the Second System." *Phi Delta Kappan* 70, 3: 248–251.

Wheatley, M.J. (1994). *Leadership and the New Science: Learning About Organization from an Orderly Universe.* San Francisco: Berrett-Koehler Publishers.

Voice of Inclusion: Developing a Shared Voice—Yours, Mine, and Ours

Nancy Keller with Lia Cravedi-Cheng

During my seven years as a middle grades science teacher in an inclusionary school district in Winooski, Vermont, I have experienced how teaching teams of general and special educators can help children of varying abilities meaningfully participate in regular classrooms.

I must confess that I was initially uneasy about the inclusion of students with physical, academic, and social challenges in my classroom. My pre-service training, although excellent at the time, had not included practical experiences within an inclusionary setting. Today, my understanding of how we can educate *all* students in the same classroom has broadened, and I realize that my initial concerns about inclusionary education really sprang from my fear of the unknown and also from not being able to visualize how this could work.

Lia, a special educator in Winooski, had a similar experience. Before she began team teaching with general educators, Lia had worked for five years as a special educator in self-contained classes and resource rooms. She was uncomfortable with sorting students by abilities, teaching them in isolation, and then expecting them to readily apply this learning in a new context. But it was "state of the art" at the time. Lia's contacts with general educators had been limited to the hellos exchanged as she pulled *her* students from other classes. Like me, Lia was also not able to visualize how students with special needs could get support otherwise. Efforts by Winooski and other school districts to integrate their teachers through teaching teams addressed this dilemma. Today, Lia and I are convinced that if teachers have adequate support and the opportunity to share their respective expertise, they can create a rich educational setting for all children.

What follows is a description of how our teaching partnership evolved, the critical elements to its success, and how it benefited our students.

The Situation

The Winooski School District serves approximately 780 students on one campus. Of these students, 14 percent are identified as having special needs. About 12 years ago, students with special needs were placed in special classes or bused to separate programs at 15 sites outside of the district. Not long after that, the district began to change its program of services for students with special needs. The on-site special schools were closed; and the students living in Winooski, but attending school elsewhere, returned to their home school.

Although students with special needs remained on campus and were included in some regular classes, the benefits of inclusionary education were not being fully realized. The dropout rate of students with disabilities was still quite high (30 percent), and their absenteeism was a chronic problem. We believed that one reason these students were reluctant to continue their education was that although physically present, they did not feel part of the school community. They were frequently pulled from their regular classrooms to receive academic coursework in a resource room, causing them to feel separate from their peers. The belief, based on years of practice, was that "special" educators had "special" skills that could target this "special" population. We faced the challenge of trying to design a learning environment in which these students would want to participate. We had only to look at our students and listen to what they were telling us—they wanted to learn alongside their friends, just like every other student.

Our administration decided that if all students were to learn side by side in a regular classroom, the teachers needed to be integrated to teach side by side. With this configuration, differences in our teacher-training backgrounds would be an asset. For example, I had been trained as a secondary science teacher, with little focus placed on making accommodations for students with learning differences. Lia, on the other hand, possessed the very skills I lacked. By combining our teaching skills, we complemented each other. Although I am not an economist, I did liken the sharing of expertise to the "trickle down" theory of economics, meaning that by working with Lia I learned strategies and techniques that supported students with special needs and positively influenced my teaching of *all* students. Ironically, Lia saw this exchange of skills from a socialist perspective: She believed that by planting seeds of change in one environment, they would eventually spread to others, and that all students would benefit over time. Looking back now, it is obvious to both of us that working in a teaming configuration was an effective way to meet the academic and social needs of both our students and ourselves.

Lia and I team-taught for two years. Unlike some teaching teams, we did not enter into our teaming relationship by choice; it was an administrative decision. And although we had not previously worked with each other at all, we have proven that this does not have to spell doom for a team. Given time and a framework for collaborating, teachers can form very effective teaching teams. This is what occurred for Lia and me. What follows is a recounting of our first two years together and strategies we found helpful.

Year 1—Developing Trust: Yours and Mine

Planning Time

Before Lia and I could stand together in front of our students and represent ourselves as a viable teaching team, we had to establish a regular planning time. Before school started in the fall, we agreed to set aside one prep period each week for planning. Because Lia and I did not know each other very well, I knew that without this initial investment of time our team would not be successful. Therefore, this became "sacred time": Both of us saw this as time that we would not allow to be interrupted by the typical demands that teachers face. And although it was just the two of us, we set an agenda for our meetings, took minutes, and assigned tasks to be completed later (e.g., prepare worksheets, make copies, talk to a student, grade papers). Teachers unwilling to invest adequate time for planning can almost guarantee they will not reach their potential in a teaching team. Notes in the mailbox or planning "on the run" do not build trusting relationships.

Division of Labor

Setting Goals. Much of this once-a-week planning time was driven by the mission our school district and our team shared—that all students would receive instruction in regular education. In addition, I set a professional goal of wanting to learn how to modify the curriculum and instruction to accomplish our larger mission. Lia's professional goal was to ensure that all the students for whom she coordinated services were successful in the regular classes. In retrospect, we can now see that establishing a common purpose and setting these clear goals provided a powerfully meaningful context in which to work.

A team can use its mission to assist its ongoing decision making by regularly asking, "Is what we are doing congruent with our mission?" For example, given that our mission was to maintain students in the regular classroom, we would look at the choice of removing a student from that environment as a last resort. Additionally, our professional goals become a yardstick by which to measure our growth as teachers. What did I learn about modifying the curriculum and instruction? Was Lia able to structure for student success, and to what degree?

Defining Roles. Although we didn't actually discuss this the first year, we both assumed from the beginning that I would be responsible for delivering the content and Lia would assist me in this endeavor. This rather conventional assumption—teacher and teaching assistant—provided the basis for dividing our labor. This meant that I took on the tasks related to what and how content would be taught, while Lia supported this instruction by classroom and student management. In other words, I identified the content to be covered, set objectives, and did the majority of lesson planning, teaching, and evaluating. Lia verbally and physically prompted students to focus on the instruction, checked their understanding, and limited off-task behavior.

We learned that the key to defining roles on a team is to consider what your students need and what expertise each educator brings to the situation. We also learned that redefining former roles requires setting egos aside. Being an assistant to the other teacher, for example, may not seem like the most glamorous job, but at times it is exactly what's needed in the classroom to serve your students' needs.

Being Accountable. Once our new roles were defined, we built further trust by following through on our commitments. After Lia had promised me that she would team with me for a minimum of one period per day, four days per week, I depended on her to be there. And I carried out my promise to clearly plan the objectives for the science lessons. If I had not upheld my part of our "deal," Lia would not have known how to support the students in my classes. The glue to this—and every—teaming relationship is accountability. (Hint: Apply this glue liberally!)

Reflection: Through the Looking Glass

One way any team continues to develop is by acknowledging accomplishments and identifying areas for further development. In our first year of teaming, we kept our reflections within the noncontroversial realm of how *our students* were doing. We avoided conversations regarding *our* performance as teachers. Although my goal was to improve my instructional skills, I did not seek feedback from Lia in this area. My fear was that I would be criticized instead of supported in the evaluation of my work. It wasn't until Lia suggested that we take a class together to focus on our teaming that I felt I could risk receiving feedback. Her invitation allowed us to revisit and redefine our goals and roles within our team.

Members of teaching teams may find reflecting on their own professional performance a scary proposition. It definitely takes trust. We enthusiastically encourage all efforts toward this evaluation goal.

Year 2—Sustaining Trust: Yours, Mine, and Ours

Reinforcement of Teaming

Lia and I were fortunate to be able to work together for a second year and, at the same time, be involved in taking coursework that helped us focus on improving our instructional skills. We were fortunate because we had a second year to develop continuity between ourselves and our students. We knew that whenever a new person is added to a team, the team must return to the early developmental stage of trust building so it can set goals, define roles, develop accountability, and work out logistics. Because our team's composition was not altered, during our second year we were able to reinforce the foundation we had built in our first year, instead of having to rebuild it with new team members. While we acknowledge that schools must be fluid when scheduling and pairing personnel from year to year, we appreciated our administrator's support of newly established teams by allowing them a second year to develop.

Planning Time

In continuing our relationship a second year, planning time remained crucial. Because we were familiar with each other and our routines, we could have become complacent about planning. The challenge for the second year, then, was to move beyond routine—to use the "lessons learned" from the previous year as a starting point for improvement. As before, regular face-to-face interaction in a structured meeting format was critical. Since "two heads are better than one," it was necessary to maintain adequate planning time as part of our routine—even if it seemed that the lessons could write themselves or the classroom could run on its own. Much could have been lost if we had let planning become incidental.

One major lesson we learned in our second year was that teams can look forward to cashing in on their first-year efforts. Such payoffs may include more efficient planning meetings, increased participation of team members, and teachers willing to go beyond and outside of their conventional roles and expertise to break new ground in content, instructional methodology, or role reversal.

Division of Labor

Revisiting Goals. We remained aware of and continued to work toward the goal of all students receiving instruction in the regular classroom. However, unlike the broad goals we had identified our first year (e.g., learning to modify curriculum and instruction), we realized that there were specific skills and strategies we needed to master to better achieve our broader goals. Specifically, we chose to jointly and systematically practice select behavior management strategies and principles of effective instruction, as well as specific accommodation strategies. This goal setting was facilitated by our involvement in our school district's inservice program. This was one way that our school district supported us as a teaching team: It provided a structured opportunity for us to experience a sense of interdependence as we worked toward our mutual goals. It helped us develop an "all for one, one for all" ethic.

Redefining Roles. As our goals became more interdependent, so did our roles. In our first year, we had defined our roles along the boundaries of our relative expertise: Lia, the special educator, and Nancy, the science teacher. In our second year, we came to see ourselves as teachers of children, not as different types of teachers for different types of children. This change of perspective significantly changed the roles that we took within the classroom. Now we were two teachers jointly responsible for developing lesson objectives, evaluating student progress, conferencing with parents, managing student behavior, and covering the logistics (e.g., making copies, preparing worksheets, setting up labs). We jointly shared the responsibilities of "classroom teacher."

We strongly recommend that all teaching teams revisit, revise, and redefine their goals and roles throughout their partnerships. The more we learn about working together, the better we get at setting specific goals and inventing more meaningful roles.

Maintaining Accountability. Accountability remained the glue that held our relationship together. I had come to expect that Lia would follow through on her responsibilities, as she had the first year. At this point, it may have been easy for both of us to occasionally neglect our commitments, thinking that "she can handle it" or "she'll understand." Given the skills we had acquired, either of us probably could have "handled it" or "understood." But our trust and effectiveness would have begun to erode. As in marriage, the challenge is to not take one another for granted, but to maintain a high level of mutual support.

Reflection: Through the Magnifying Glass

During our second year of working together, Lia and I continued to reflect on student performance, considering this an initially safe topic. However, as a result of our having developed a high level of trust, we also began to discuss our teaching and our progress as a team. This discussion, which at times was difficult, yielded tremendous results for us individually and as a team, including increased trust and risk-taking for the sake of our students.

Successful blending of all students in general education classrooms happens when support is provided to both students and teachers. Giving general and special educators the opportunity to share their respective expertise as a teaching team opens the door to a richer educational experience for all children. Students previously taught in more isolated settings can achieve in the regular classroom and also avoid the stigma associated with being "pulled out." Students of all abilities can learn and reach their potential together in the same class.

As teachers, Lia and I have realized the importance of "sacred" planning time, goal setting, role redefinition, personal accountability, and reflection in successfully merging professional talent and skills for the benefit of our students. We have also realized the great social and professional benefits that accrue from two professionals working closely together. By working as a team, members benefit by sharing both the challenges and the fun. Lia now has numerous relationships with general educators to replace the passing hellos at the doorway. And I no longer experience teaching as an isolated professional, for I now appreciate the critical part my colleagues play in my professional growth.

5

Promising Practices That Foster Inclusive Education

Alice Udvari-Solner and Jacqueline S. Thousand

The inclusive education movement has often been viewed as a separate initiative running parallel or even counter to other curricular and instructional reform efforts (Block and Haring 1992). We take a holistic rather than separatist viewpoint and propose that the innovative changes occurring in general education are the same kinds of changes required for effective inclusion.

A number of established and emerging general education practices emulate the principles of inclusive education. When these practices are used, educators may be better equipped to facilitate meaningful and effective inclusive education for students perceived as disabled, at risk, or gifted, as well as those considered "average." Among the initiatives that have great promise for building inclusive schools are outcome-based education, multicultural education, multiple intelligence theory, constructivist learning, interdisciplinary curriculum, community-referenced instruction, authentic assessment of student performance, multi-age grouping, use of technology in the classroom, peer-mediated instruction, teaching responsibility and peacemaking, and collaborative teaming among adults and students. The remainder of this chapter examines each practice in the light of inclusive education.

Outcome-Based Education

Outcome-based education (OBE) is not a new concept to educators; it has evolved over the past 40 years to its current conceptualization with three central premises (Spady and Marshall 1991):

• All children can learn and succeed, although not in the same way or on the same day.
• Success breeds success.
• Schools determine the conditions of success.

In addition, OBE is guided by four principles (Brandt 1992–1993). The first, *clarity of focus,* implies that all aspects of education (curriculum, instruction, assessment) are centered on what we want children to demonstrate by the end of their schooling career (for example, the Circle of Courage outcomes of belonging, mastery, independence, and generosity discussed in Chapter 3). Everyone is clear at all times about the goals of education.

The second principle, *expanding opportunity,* recognizes that students learn in different ways and at different rates, and that various methods and contexts (perhaps out of the school building) are needed to optimize learning. Outcome demonstration is not tied to the calendar.

The third principle, *high expectations,* is rooted in the assumption that every student is "able to do significant things well" (Bill Spady, quoted by Brandt 1992–1993, p. 66). All students are expected to demonstrate success in their own way.

Finally, the fourth principle, *designing down,* turns the traditional method of designing curriculum upside down. Long-range outcomes are established first, and then curriculum is designed, always with an eye on where students ultimately are expected to end up.

Why institute OBE for students with disabilities? Clearly, OBE is consistent with and supportive of an inclusive education philosophy. OBE professes to encompass all students and focus on success for all. Additionally, many community members and education leaders are attracted to the autonomy schools are given to establish the means—the curriculum—for achieving significant outcomes. Teachers are encouraged to be flexible and to provide educational experiences in a variety of ways for a diverse student body. Students are not required to do the same things in the same ways in the same amount of time as same-aged peers.

Some question how students with severe disabilities can be included in OBE. McLaughlin and Warren (1992) argue that students with intensive challenges can be a part of the OBE model if the curriculum is defined in broad and balanced areas of knowledge and skill rather than narrow subject areas. To illustrate, 4,000 adults and students provided input into the development of Vermont's Common Core of Learning (Vermont State Department of Education 1993). The Common Core identified these skills as vital results: communication, reasoning and problem solving, personal development, social responsibility, and fields of knowledge including technology and new disciplines that "may be only just coming into existence" (p. 12).

Clearly, students with severe disabilities can achieve in many of these vital domains, although the performance criteria and method of assessing success may be quite different from that of their classmates. Central to this question is the notion of "personal best" (Shriner, Ysseldyke, Thurlow, and Honetschlager 1994, p. 41). For example, literacy may be an expectation for all graduates. One student demonstrates his personal best by writing a persuasive speech, whereas another demonstrates her personal best by effectively using her assistive communication device to express her wants and interests.

Multicultural Education

The term *multicultural education* has been used to describe various policies related to educational equity and practices that foster understanding of human differences and similarities (Banks and McGee Banks 1989, Sleeter and Grant 1994). The principles of multiculturalism were formulated in the 1960s and '70s as issues of culture and diversity rose to the forefront of political and educational arenas. Initially, these principles were most prominently associated with gender, ethnicity, and class distinctions. Only recently have the issues of disability and sexual orientation made their way into the multicultural literature (Tiedt and Tiedt 1990). As a result, multicultural education has rarely been linked effectively with inclusive education.

When the underlying goals of a multicultural approach are examined, they fit well with the ideological framework of inclusive education. The goals and outcomes of multicultural education are to:

- foster human rights and respect for difference,
- acknowledge the value of cultural diversity,
- promote an understanding of alternative life choices,
- establish social justice and equal opportunity, and
- facilitate equitable power distribution among individuals and groups (Gollnick 1980).

When school communities employ a multicultural approach, they make a commitment to empower students and to attempt to increase academic achievement by redesigning the entire educational agenda to make learning environments responsive to students' cultures, behavior, and learning styles (Banks and McGee Banks 1989).

Grant and Sleeter (1989) have extended the concept of multicultural education using a *reconstructionist* viewpoint. Simply stated, reconstructionism requires a critique of contemporary culture and a reconceptualization of what it can and should be to realize a more humane society (Brameld 1956). Students are encouraged to critically evaluate inequities and instances of discrimination or bias and to identify strategies for change. By engaging in a meta-analysis of existing conditions and establishing visions that reflect a value system, even the youngest members of school communities are encouraged to make a personal commitment to change. A reconstructionist orientation holds promise for accelerating educational reform by embedding reformation in teachers' and students' day-to-day discourse.

Although multicultural education and inclusion are not synonymous, administrators, educators, and community members need to recognize the commonalities between them so they may coordinate reform activities within schools to maximize the use of resources and optimize the number of children who will benefit.

Multiple Intelligences Theory

The theory of multiple intelligences (MI-theory) proposed by Howard Gardner (1983) questions the adequacy and efficacy of the traditional conceptualization of knowledge, aptitude, and intellect. As defined in the western world, intelligence has long been equated with logical and linguistic abilities. The underlying assumptions of this view are that the processes of the mind are quantifiable and can be translated into a singular construct. Furthermore, all children can be compared and rank ordered by intellectual prowess (Goldman and Gardner 1989), hence our reliance on I.Q. scores as essential descriptors of students' abilities and predictors of academic success.

MI-theory is based on the supposition that several distinct forms or families of intelligence exist—or, more accurately, co-exist—to create a constellation of ability for any one individual. Gardner (1983) has recommended consideration of at least seven types of intelligence: linguistic, logical-mathematical, musical, spatial, bodily-kinesthetic, interpersonal, and intrapersonal.

These categories are constructed to promote the valuing of skills beyond the conventional representations of verbal ability, written expression, and mathematical reasoning. Gardner's valued capacities include: the ability to depict and manipulate spatial representations; to think in and produce musical forms; to use kinesthetic action to perform, produce, and problem solve; and to use effective communication and interaction skills to understand others or reflect on one's own behavior.

The notion of multiple intelligences has important implications for inclusive education. Gardner based his theory in part on observations and studies of the capacities of children with disabilities and on the meaning of intelligence in varied cultures (Gardner 1983), thus validating a broader perspective. Teachers equipped with this perspective are in the position to appreciate students' "unconventional" behavior and seek productive applications of these skills within a learning context. They will arrange learning activities to allow expression of knowledge through multiple modes and the use of different intelligences. Teachers may use the student's strongest modalities or intelligences as vehicles to promote skill acquisition in weaker areas of performance.

MI-theory does not allow the student to be viewed only through the constricted lens of logic or language. Instead, learning and memory are seen as multifaceted and not completely understood. Consequently, our mechanisms for assessing intelligence are at the very least far too narrow and perhaps misguided. This calls into question the current systems used to identify and label any child as disabled. Embracing the tenets of MI-theory could interrupt the vicious cycle of labeling and the social construction of disability based on one or two aspects of ability.

The use of a multiple-intelligence orientation liberates educators to see the idiosyncrasies in learning styles and differentiate curriculum for all students, thus making "difference" usual in the classroom.

Constructivist Learning

From a constructivist perspective, learning is the creation of meaning when an individual makes linkages between new knowledge and the context of existing knowledge (Poplin and Stone 1992). A key characteristic of this view, then, is that learners "construct" their own knowledge (Peterson, Fennema, and Carpenter 1988–1989). Generally speaking, the ideas of Brownwell, Vygotsky, Dewey, and Piaget are constructivist (Resnick and Klopfer 1989); underpinning their theories is the idea that knowledge is not quantitative but interpretive and must develop in social contexts of communities and communicative interchanges (Peterson and Knapp 1993).

Constructivism challenges the assumptions and practices of reductionism that have pervaded our educational practices for generations. In a deficit-driven reductionist framework, effective learning takes place in a rigid, hierarchical progression. Each concept or skill is broken into small segments or steps, and students learn each one in sequence (Poplin and Stone 1992). A supposition exists that children are unable to learn higher-order skills before mastering those of lower order (Peterson et al. 1988–1989). Learning, then, is an accumulation of isolated facts. It is presumed that through this accumulation process, learners will build skills and generate new knowledge.

Conceptualizing curriculum and instruction from a constructivist vantage point intersects productively with the practices of inclusive education. Constructivism fosters the idea that all people are always learning, and the process cannot be stopped (Poplin and Stone 1992). "No human being understands everything; every human being understands some thing. Education should strive to improve understanding as much as possible, whatever the student's proclivities might be" (Siegel and Shaughnessy 1994, p. 564). Both of these statements imply that there are few, if any, prerequisites for learning and that children must be met at their current level of performance without undue focus on remediation. It is acknowledged that all students enter school with different knowledge that is influenced by background, experiences, and cultural practice. Consequently, teachers must take into account these factors and ensure that new information is related in meaningful ways to each learner's existing knowledge.

Interdisciplinary Curriculum

An interdisciplinary approach is a curricular orientation that expressly employs methodology and language from more than one discipline to examine a central theme, issue, problem, topic, or experience (Jacobs 1989). Teachers and students are encouraged in a learning partnership to examine one area in depth from complex and multiple perspectives. Interdisciplinary curriculum may be implemented in several ways. At the elementary level, a single teacher can interface the content of assorted disciplines throughout one unit of study. Instructors of art, music, and physical education can further infuse the theme across the instructional day. Most true to the interdisciplinary philosophy is the practice at middle and high school levels of uniting teachers of separate disciplines to team teach around a selected set of issues.

Interdisciplinary/thematic approaches have grown out of dissatisfaction with discipline-based or subject-driven methods of curriculum organization. Discipline-based models are premised on the teaching of content knowledge. However, knowledge in all areas of study is growing exponentially each day. Essentially, there are not enough hours in the day to teach all that is new. Jacobs (1989) believes this indicates a need to rethink the way we select areas of study, deciding not only what should be taught, but what should be eliminated. Fragmentation of schedules and subject matter into allotted time periods is common practice in discipline-based approaches. With thematic methods, students are not forced to create bridges among seemingly unrelated splinters of information but instead can view issues in a holistic manner.

If discipline-based approaches pose drawbacks for the typical population, the impact on students with disabilities is likely to be more significant. One reason students with disabilities failed in the past in general education classes was that the subject matter presented was unrelated, out of context, and practiced only a few minutes per day without consideration for generalization and transfer. A thematic orientation offers a way to show how different subject areas relate and influence students' lives, thereby affirming the relevance of the curriculum (Ackerman and Perkins 1989, Bean 1990).

Community-Referenced Instruction

Community-referenced or community-based instruction is characterized by students applying skills in nonschool settings that have some relationship, relevance, and purpose to their lives now or in the future (Falvey 1989). Instruction takes place regularly in community environments where age-appropriate vocational, domestic, community, or recreational skills can be acquired (Brown, Branston, Baumgart, Vincent, Falvey, and Schroeder 1979). The premise behind community-referenced instruction is that all students need an education that prepares them with the skills to live and work as part of the adult community—in other words, to achieve functional outcomes (Clark 1994).

A community-based approach to instruction evolved as a best practice for students with moderate and severe disabilities (Brown et al. 1979). However, it is now recognized as a valuable tool in the education of all students (Peterson, LeRoy, Field, and Wood 1992). Given the complexities of adult life in the 21st century, educators are realizing that all the skills that are relevant, critical, and enriching cannot be taught effectively within the confines of the classroom. For students with significant disabilities who may experience problems generalizing skills acquired in one setting to another, the need for systematic instruction in the actual environment of concern is evident. For students without disabilities, there is a need to connect with the larger community, work in concert with community members to engage in problem-solving skills, and integrate themselves as participants in businesses and organizations long before graduation occurs.

Accessing the community for instruction can provide a student with disabilities the context to learn or maintain a new skill. The same environment can be used as a "fidelity check" for the application of math, science, or language skills for typical students. For example, each week a group of three students from a 7th grade home economics class goes to the local grocery store. For the member of the group who has disabilities, the weekly trip serves as an opportunity to learn to travel by city bus, cross streets, and select and pay for groceries. The other students in the group must use mathematics and nutrition skills by comparative shopping to select items that are most economical and contain the least grams of fat, thus employing skills emphasized within the classroom.

Authentic Assessment of Student Performance

The need for better alignment between assessment and instruction is even more evident (Chittenden 1991) as schools have begun to shift their curriculum to include multicultural, constructivist, interdisciplinary, and community-referenced approaches, and as teachers have placed more emphasis on the meaning of learning with attention to children's interests and proclivities. Traditional measures of performance that do not provide information about students' understanding and quality of thinking are out of step with dynamic, student-centered instructional practices.

Perrone (1994) noted that typical assessment techniques relying primarily on the recall of knowledge provide an artificial, decontextualized view of the learner. Assessment has been equated with the possession of information rather than the acquisition of global constructs (e.g., learning the process of writing) (Zessoules and Gardner 1991). In most cases, data acquired from these assessments are unrelated to the ways students naturally learn or will need to use the knowledge. This problem is amplified for students with disabilities. When traditional measures such as standardized, norm-referenced tests are used for evaluation, their performances predictably fall below those of their nondisabled peers. Thus, a unidimensional and deficit-oriented profile of the learner is maintained.

Based on the need for more realistic and responsive outcome measures, a number of alternative evaluation techniques—authentic assessments—have evolved. Authentic assessment occurs when students are expected to perform, produce, or otherwise demonstrate skills that represent realistic learning demands (Choate and Evans 1992, Diez and Moon 1992). According to Meyer (1992), the contexts of the assessments are real-life settings in and out of the classroom without contrived and standardized conditions. Authentic assessments can be considered exhibitions of learning that are gathered over time to show evidence of progress, acquisition, and application. For example, written expression may be assessed through the use of a portfolio that includes several samples of writing representing conceptual ideas, rough drafts, self-edited papers, and final versions. Included in this assessment may be products such as poems, letters, or research papers that illustrate ability to use other forms of written expression. The student also is encouraged to include self-evaluations and personal goals for progress.

Common features of authentic assessments are:

• Students must integrate and apply skills to accomplish a larger task (Choate and Evans 1992).

• The processes of learning, higher-level thinking, or problem-solving are emphasized, as well as the product of these actions (Diez and Moon 1992).

• Assessment tasks must help students make judgments about their own performance. Through self-appraisal, children set goals for progress and provoke further learning (Perrone 1994, Zessoules and Gardner 1991).

• The criteria for performance are negotiated and made explicit to students in advance (Wiggins 1989).

The use of authentic assessments is an important component in creating inclusive classrooms. This form of evaluation is closely linked to the individualized, performance-based assessment that has been the preferred mode of assessment in special education. These techniques are less likely to be culturally biased for students who are limited in English proficiency or in any other intellectual, physical, or emotional capacity.

Students with unique learning characteristics and their peers are allowed to express knowledge through multiple modes and in nontraditional ways (Perrone 1991). Instruction and assessments are provided with relevant tasks so students who have difficulty generalizing skills or using them out of context are not required to transfer learnings to demonstrate understanding (Choate and Evans 1992). Functional expressions of competence more readily enable teachers to identify skills that are discrepant or mastered, thus giving direction to instruction of highest priority.

Multi-Age Grouping

Kasten and Clarke (1993) define multi-age grouping as "any deliberate grouping of children that includes more than one traditional grade level in a single classroom community" (p. 3). Also referred to as nongraded, family, or vertical grouping, multi-age classrooms are considered single learning communities made up of a balanced collection of students from the school population with consideration for heterogeneity in gender, ability, ethnicity, interests, and age levels. It is not unlikely to have siblings and members of the extended family within one vertical grouping.

The multi-age classroom, a well-established practice in countries such as Canada, New Zealand, Britain, and some parts of the United States (Elkind 1987), is based on several underlying assumptions that directly oppose the traditional practice of grade-level grouping. Grade-level grouping presumes that students who are the same age have like learning needs and abilities, thus benefiting from similar instruction. Placement of the child is based solely on age or physical time (Elkind 1987). Learning by grade level is viewed as a predictable, sequential, and orderly procedure; and one year of schooling is a product that can be judged and rated by a standard of performance (Kasten and Clark 1993).

In contrast, a multi-age approach is based on the assumption that learning is a continuous and dynamic process. Student diversity is essential. Children are expected and, in fact, encouraged to learn at different rates and levels. The growth of the child is viewed in both biological and psychological time, rather than merely physical time, so that learning experiences are designed as developmentally appropriate.

Many elements of multi-age grouping that work for students without disabilities are also advantageous for students with disabilities. The emphasis on *heterogeneity* requires a classroom organization flexible enough to accommodate children at different levels of maturity and with different levels of intellectual ability. In fact, diversity impedes the use of lock-step instructional methods aimed at the whole class or a specific grade level.

The sense of *community* created over time among teachers and students is advantageous to promote long-term networks of support for students with disabilities. Transitions from setting to setting and teacher to teacher are associated with recoupment, generalization, and social adjustment difficulties for some students with disabilities. These "passages" are reduced in nongraded groupings, and teachers have time to get to know a particular student. Teachers can use information gained about the child in one year to plan learning experiences for the next year without the risk of losing that knowledge in a transition to new staff.

Use of Technology in the Classroom

Technology is proving to be a catalyst for transforming schooling by fostering excitement in learning for all children. As Peck and Dorricott of the Institute for the Reinvention of Education (1994) observed:

> To see students so engaged in learning that they lose track of time, to see a level of excitement that causes students to come to school early and stay late, and to have time to develop strong relationships with students and to meet their individual needs allows educators to fulfill age-old dreams (p. 14).

What is technology? It is more than computers and software packages, and it reinvents itself almost daily. Technology in education includes calculators, video cameras, VCRs, portable personal computers, printers, general-purpose software such as word processing programs and *HyperCard*, computer-assisted instruction for drill and practice, laser videodisks, telecommunication networks such as electronic mail, distance education, interactive multimedia, scanners, text-to-speech and speech-to-text software, pen-based notepads such as the Apple *Newton*, and more. Given the current and expanding access to technology inside and outside of the classroom, the climate is conducive to including students with disabilities who need technology to access the curriculum, express their knowledge, communicate, or control their environment.

In the past, technology was only in the possession of a few experts such as the computer lab teacher or those who designed or programmed augmentative communication systems for students with communication limitations. Today, technology has become "user friendly." Educators are joining the ranks of adults and children who rarely go a day without interacting with their laptop computer for desktop publishing, data management, game playing, or instantly communicating and socializing via the Internet.

Technological tools of a student with disabilities that once seemed too complex, cumbersome, or expensive (for example, massive computers bolted to a table or voice synthesizers) have become very portable, affordable, and standard hardware and software features of schools. Technology that used to be unusual for a single student now is usual within the classroom. Never before have educators been in such an ideal position to capitalize on technological advances in order to readily educate students who have different learning styles and rates or who rely on technological support to learn, communicate, and control their world.

In an interview with Frank Betts (1994), David Thornburg laid out a scenario that would equip every 2nd or 3rd grade child with a "loaded" computer for $100 per child. For $200, the system could be upgraded in 8th grade. But he cautions that even with the feasibility for advanced technology at every child's fingertips at home and school, equipment and software does not guarantee an excellent educational program (Thornburg 1992). Teachers still need to get to know each child and base decisions on how each child learns. Commenting on the use of technology to support the inclusion and learning of students with disabilities in school, Dutton and Dutton (1990) state it this way:

> Remember that technology is not a "cure" for a disability; rather, it is a tool for everyone in society. Focus should not be placed on how the equipment itself will work, but efforts should be placed toward developing strategies, utilizing effective teaching practices, and working with the strengths of all students in the class. Technology can help remove barriers, but it is people, working together, who learn and succeed (p. 182).

Chapter 6 offers a process for interprofessional collaboration to adapt curriculum and instruction that may include the use of technology to meet individual student needs.

Peer-Mediated Instruction

"Peer-mediated instruction" (Harper, Maheady, and Mallette 1994, p. 229) refers to any teaching arrangement in which students serve as instructional agents for other students. Cooperative group-learning models and peer tutoring or partner learning strategies are two forms of peer-mediated instruction that support inclusive education.

As Johnson and Johnson (1994) point out, students may interact in three ways during learning. They may compete to see who is the best, they may work alone and individually toward their goals without attending to other students, or they may have a stake in one another's success by working cooperatively. Competitive learning interferes with community building, which is one objective of inclusive education. Yet, "research indicates that a vast majority of students in the United States view school as a competitive enterprise where one tries to do better than other students" (Johnson and Johnson 1994, pp. 32–33).

It is critical to note the dramatic difference between simply asking students to sit together and work in a group, and careful structuring so students work in cooperative learning groups. A group of children chatting together at a table as they do their own work is not a cooperative group, because no sense of positive interdependence exists, and no need for mutual support is arranged for them. It is only under particular conditions that groups will have healthy and productive relationships and may be expected to be more productive than in individualistic or competitive learning arrangements. Common to the diverse approaches of cooperative learning are five conditions or attributes:

- a joint task or learning activity suitable for group work,
- small-group learning in teams of five or fewer members,
- a focus on cooperative interpersonal behaviors,
- positive interdependence through team members' encouragement of one another's learning, and
- individual responsibility and accountability for the participation and learning of each team member (Davidson 1994).

A rich research base supports the use of cooperative learning to facilitate successful learning in heterogeneous groupings of students with varying abilities, interests, and backgrounds. Within the context of inclusive education, cooperative learning makes great sense as an instructional strategy as it enables students "to learn and work in environments where their individual strengths are recognized and individual needs are addressed" (Sapon-Shevin, Ayres, and Duncan 1994, p. 46). In other words, cooperative learning allows the classroom to be transformed into a microcosm of the diverse society and work world into which students will enter and a place for acquiring the skills to appreciate and cope with people who initially might be perceived as different or even difficult. Within this context, students learn what a society in which each person is valued would be like.

Partner learning or peer tutoring systems are not new; teachers of one-room school houses relied heavily on students as instructors. Children are continually teaching one another informally when they play games and engage in sports. Partner learning systems build relationships among students and offer a cost-effective way of enhancing engaged learning time on the part of children. Peer tutor systems can be same-age or cross-age and can be established within a single classroom, across classes, or across an entire school. Evidence of the social, instructional, and cost effectiveness of tutoring continues to mount (e.g., Fuchs, Fuchs, Hamlett, Phillips, and Bentz 1994; Thousand, Villa, and Nevin 1994). Benefits to students receiving this type of instruction include learning gains, interpersonal skill development, and heightened self-esteem. Good and Brophy (1987) suggest the quality of instruction provided by trained tutors may be superior to that of adults for at least three reasons:

- Children use more age-appropriate and meaningful language and examples.
- Having recently learned what they are to teach, they are familiar with their partner's potential frustrations.
- They tend to be more direct than adults.

Tutors also experience benefits similar to those of their partners. Namely, they develop interpersonal skills and may enhance self-esteem. Further, tutors report that they understand the concepts, procedures, and operations they teach at a much deeper level than they did before instructing. This likely is due to their meta-cognitive activity when preparing to teach.

Teaching Responsibility and Peacemaking

Among the children who are perceived as the most challenging to educate within current school organizational structures are those who demonstrate high rates of rule-violating behavior, children who have acquired maladaptive ways of relating, and children who are perceived as troubled or troubling. Adversity at home and in the community negatively affects an increasing number of children's ability and motivation to learn. The educator's job has broadened from providing effective and personalized learning opportunities to addressing the stressors in children's lives by offering a variety of school-based social supports (for example, breakfast program, free lunch, mental health, and other human services on campus). Personal responsibility and peacemaking have risen to the top as curriculum priorities (Villa, Udis, and Thousand 1994).

Educators long have recognized that for students to master a content area such as mathematics or science, they need continuous and complex instruction throughout their elementary, middle, and high school years. When a child does not grasp concept or skill, we react with a "teaching response" and attempt to reteach the material with additional or different supports and accommodations. The content area of responsibility, however, has not received the same immediate treatment. The explicit teaching of patterns of behavior and habits representative of responsible behavior often never occurs. Instead, instruction is relegated to reactive, add on, quick-fix methods such as seeing a guidance counselor, going to a six-week social skills group, or instituting a written behavior change plan. To teach responsibility is as demanding as teaching any other content; it requires careful thought and complex, ongoing instruction from the day a child enters school.

Requisite to students learning responsible values, attitudes, and behaviors is the perception that somebody in the school community genuinely cares about them. Thus, teachers, above all, must demonstrate caring and concern by validating students' efforts and achievements. They must also directly teach responsibility by setting limits to ensure safety; establishing a schoolwide discipline system that promotes the learning of responsibility; and directly instructing students in pro-social communication skills, anger management, and impulse control techniques (Villa et al. 1994).

Models of discipline that are responsibility based (Curwin and Mendler 1988, Glasser 1986) acknowledge conflict as a natural part of life. They consider behavior to be contextual and transform the educator's role from cop to facilitator. There are no "if-then" consequences (e.g., three tardies equals a detention; 10 absences results in a grade of "F" in the missed class). Instead, responses to rule-violating behavior depend on all kinds of factors such as the time of day, the frequency and intensity of the behavior, and the number of other people exhibiting the behavior. These responses range from reminders, warnings, re-directions, cues, and self-monitoring techniques to behavioral contracts and direct teaching of alternative responses. Most important is to recognize that the development of student responsibility should be part of the curriculum and considered as important as any other curriculum domain. It should be concerned with teaching young people how to get their needs met in socially acceptable ways and should include modeling, coaching, and ongoing thought and reflection on the part of school personnel.

One way to incorporate the development of student responsibility into the curriculum and culture of a school is to turn conflict management back to the students by using them as peer mediators. In an increasing number of North American schools, students are trained to mediate conflicts and are available during school hours to conduct mediations at student, teacher, or administrator request. A small number of students may be selected and trained in mediation processes or all students may receive training in conflict resolutions skills. Students who serve as mediators sometimes are called peacemakers or conflict managers.

Schrumpf (1994) outlined a structured process for establishing a peer mediation program within a school. He emphasizes that peer mediation must be made highly visible so students and teachers actually use the program as an alternative to adult intervention. Mediators need ongoing adult support through regular meetings in which they discuss issues and receive advanced training. Data collection in the form of Peer Mediation Requests and Peer Mediation Agreements are analyzed to determine the nature, frequency, and outcomes of mediation requests.

Emerging data suggest that peer mediation programs correlate with improved school attendance and decreases in fights, student suspensions, and vandalism. For example, of the 130 teachers in a New York City school in which students practiced peer mediation, 71 percent reported reductions in physical violence, 66 percent heard less verbal harassment, and 69 percent observed increased student willingness to cooperate with one another (Meek 1992). Learning to resolve conflicts with peers is an empowering action consistent with the principles of inclusive education, with the potential of generalizing from peace between two people to peacemaking in community and global contexts.

Collaborative Teaming Among Adults and Students

As emphasized in the preceding chapter, schools showing great success in responding to student diversity have redefined the role of general and special educators and other support personnel to that of collaborative team members who assemble to jointly problem solve the daily challenges of heterogeneous schooling. Among the benefits of collaborative planning and teaching team arrangements is the increased instructor/learner ratio and the resulting immediacy in diagnosing and responding to individual student's needs. Teaming arrangements capitalize on the diverse knowledge and instructional strengths of each team member and, when special educators are included on the team, eliminate the need to refer students to special education in order to access special educators' support. Although "collaborative teaming" is not yet the norm in North American schools, when the term is discussed, it generally conjures up images of adults (usually professional educators, sometimes community members) sharing planning, teaching, and evaluation responsibilities. Until recently, the students themselves were missing from the teaming concept.

Villa and Thousand (1992) have identified multiple rationales for including students in collaborative educational roles with adults. First, students represent a wealthy pool of expertise, refreshing creativity, and enthusiasm at no cost to schools. Second, educational reform recommendations call for students to exercise higher-level thinking skills to determine what, where, when, and how they will learn. Third, collaborating with adults in advocacy efforts for other learners helps students develop the ethic and practice of contributing to and caring for a greater community and society. Fourth, given the information explosion and the complexity of our networked global community, collaborative teaming skills are necessary for survival in the workplace. Educators, then, have a responsibility to model collaboration by sharing their decision-making and instructional power with students and arranging for and inviting students to join in at least the following collaborative endeavors (Villa and Thousand 1992):

• Students as members of teaching teams and as instructors in cooperative learning and partner learning arrangements.

• Students as members of planning teams, determining accommodations for themselves or classmates with and without disabilities.

• Students functioning as advocates for themselves and for classmates during meetings (e.g., individual educational plan meeting for a student with a disability) and other major events that determine a student's future educational and post-school choices.

• Students as mediators of conflict.

• Students providing social and logistical support to a classmate as a peer partner or a member of a Circle of Friends (Falvey, Forest, Pearpoint, and Rosenberg 1994).

• Students as coaches of their teachers, offering feedback regarding the effectiveness of their instructional and discipline procedures and decisions.

• Students as members of inservice, curriculum, discipline, and other school governance committees such as the school board.

All of these options for collaboration facilitate meaningful inclusion and participation of students with disabilities in school. Asking students to join with adults in collaborative action is a critical strategy for fostering the spirit of community and equity that is foundational to quality heterogeneous schooling experiences and the desired educational outcomes of active student participation and critical thinking.

❧   ❧   ❧

The exemplary and promising practices identified in this chapter establish the infrastructure within which the principles of inclusive education can be realized. Collectively, the initiatives have the potential to a create a unified philosophy and revolutionary standards of educational practice. The success of any change, however, always relies on the courage and determination of practicing educators to translate and put in place principles of these contemporary reform initiatives. "You can't mandate what matters," Fullan writes (1993, p. 125); instead, the complex goals of change require knowledge, skills, collaboration, creative thinking, and committed and passionate action. If widespread progress is ever to occur in education, inclusive education must not be treated as an "add on" to other pressing initiatives; it must be the central discussion, and teachers must be the central participants in a scholarly discourse on education's future. The interface between inclusive education and other exemplary practices must become clearly and publicly self-evident (Peterson and Knapp 1993).

References

Ackerman, D., and D.N. Perkins. (1989). "Integrating Thinking and Learning Skills Across the Curriculum." In *Interdisciplinary Curriculum: Design and Implementation,* edited by H.H. Jacobs. Alexandria Va: Association for Supervision and Curriculum Development.

Banks, J., and C. McGee Banks. (1989). *Multicultural Education: Issues and Perspectives.* Boston: Allyn and Bacon.

Bean, J. (May 1990). "Rethinking the Middle School Curriculum." *Middle School Journal* 21, 5: 1–5.

Betts, F. (1994). "On the Birth of the Communication Age: A Conversation with David Thornburg." *Educational Leadership* 51, 7: 20–23.

Block, J.H., and T.G. Haring. (1992). "On Swamps, Bogs, Alligators and Special Education Reform." In *Restructuring for a Caring and Effective Education: An*

Administrative Guide to Creating Heterogeneous Education, edited by R. Villa, J. Thousand, W. Stainback, and S. Stainback. Baltimore: Paul H. Brookes.

Brameld, T. (1956). *Toward a Reconstructed Philosophy of Education.* New York: Holt, Rinehart, and Winston.

Brandt, R. (1992–1993). "A Conversation with Bill Spady." *Educational Leadership* 50, 4: 66–70.

Brown, L., M. Branston, D. Baumgart, L. Vincent, M. Falvey, and J. Schroeder. (1979). "Utilizing the Characteristics of Current and Subsequent Environments as Factors in the Development of Curricular Content for Severely Handicapped Students." *AAESPH Review* 4, 4: 407–424.

Chittenden, E. (1991). "Authentic Assessment, Evaluation, and Documentation." In *Expanding Student Assessment,* edited by V. Perrone. Alexandria, Va.: Association for Supervision and Curriculum Development.

Choate, J.S., and S. Evans. (1992). "Authentic Assessment of Special Learners: Problem or Promise?" *Preventing School Failure* 37, 1: 6–9.

Clark, G. (1994). "Is Functional Curriculum Approach Compatible with an Inclusive Education Model?" *Teaching Exceptional Children* 26, 2: 36–37.

Curwin, R., and A. Mendler. (1988). *Discipline with Dignity.* Alexandria, Va.: Association for Supervision and Curriculum Development.

Davidson, N. (1994). "Cooperative and Collaborative Learning: An Integrated Perspective." In *Creativity and Collaborative Learning: A Practical Guide to Empowering Students and Teachers,* edited by J. Thousand, R. Villa, and A. Nevin. Baltimore: Paul H. Brookes.

Diez, M., and J. Moon. (1992). "What Do We Want Students to Know? . . . And Other Important Questions." *Educational Leadership* 49, 8: 38–41.

Dutton, D.H., and D.L. Dutton. (1990). "Technology to Support Diverse Needs in Regular Classes." In *Support Networks for Inclusive Schooling: Interdependent Integrated Education,* edited by W. Stainback and S. Stainback. Baltimore: Paul H. Brookes.

Elkind, D. (1987). "Multiage Grouping." *Young Children* 43, 11: 2.

Falvey, M.A. (1989). *Community Based Curriculum: Instructional Strategies for Students with Severe Handicaps.* Baltimore: Paul H. Brookes.

Falvey, M.A., M. Forest, J. Pearpoint, and R.L. Rosenberg. (1994). "Building Connections." In *Creativity and Collaborative Learning: A Practical Guide to Empowering Students and Teachers,* edited by J. Thousand, R. Villa, and A. Nevin. Baltimore: Paul H. Brookes.

Ford, A., R. Schnorr, L. Meyer, L. Davern, J. Black, and P. Dempsey. (1989). *The Syracuse Community-Referenced Curriculum Guide for Students with Moderate and Severe Disabilities.* Baltimore: Paul H. Brookes.

Fuchs, L.S., D. Fuchs, C.L. Hamlett, N.B. Phillips, and J. Bentz. (1994). "Classwide Curriculum-Based Measurement: Helping General Educators Meet the Challenge of Student Diversity." *Exceptional Children* 60: 518–537.

Fullan, M. (1993). "Innovative Reform and Restructuring Strategies." In *Challenges and Achievements of American Education*, edited by G. Cawelti. 1993 ASCD Yearbook. Alexandria, Va.: Association for Supervision and Curriculum Development.

Gardner, H. (1983). *Frames of Mind: The Theory of Multiple Intelligences.* New York: Harper Collins Publishers.

Glasser, W. (1986). *Control Theory in the Classroom.* New York: Harper and Row.

Goldman, J., and H. Gardner. (1989). "Multiple Paths to Educational Effectiveness." In *Beyond Separate Education: Quality Education for All*, edited by D.K. Lipskey and A. Gartner. Baltimore: Paul H. Brookes.

Gollnick, D.M. (1980). "Multicultural Education." *Viewpoints in Teaching and Learning* 56: 1–17.

Good, T.L., and J.G. Brophy. (1987). *Looking into Classrooms*, 4th ed. New York: Harper & Row.

Grant, C., and C. Sleeter. (1989). "Race, Class, Gender, Exceptionality, and Educational Reform." In *Multicultural Education: Issues and Perspectives*, edited by J. Banks and C. McGee Banks. Boston: Allyn and Bacon.

Harper, G.F., L. Maheady, and B. Mallette. (1994). "The Power of Peer-Mediated Instruction: How and Why It Promotes Academic Success for All Students." In *Creativity and Collaborative Learning: A Practical Guide to Empowering Students and Teachers*, edited by J. Thousand, R. Villa, and A. Nevin. Baltimore: Paul H. Brookes.

Jacobs, H.H. (1989). "The Growing Need for Interdisciplinary Curriculum Content." In *Interdisciplinary Curriculum: Design and Implementation*, edited by H.H. Jacobs. Alexandria Va.: Association for Supervision and Curriculum Development.

Johnson, R.T., and D.W. Johnson. (1994). "An Overview of Cooperative Learning." In *Creativity and Collaborative Learning: A Practical Guide to Empowering Students and Teachers*, edited by J. Thousand, R. Villa, and A. Nevin. Baltimore: Paul H. Brookes.

Kasten, W., and B. Clarke. (1993). *The Multi-age Classroom: A Family of Learners.* Katonah, N.Y.: Richard C. Owen Publishers.

McLaughlin, M., and S. Warren. (1992). *Issues and Options in Restructuring Schools and Special Education Programs.* College Park: University of Maryland, The Center for Policy Options in Special Education, and the Institute for the Study of Exceptional Children and Youth.

Meek, M. (Fall 1992). "The Peacekeepers." *Teaching Tolerance*, pp. 46–52.

Meyer, C. (1992). "What's the Difference Between Authentic and Performance Assessment?" *Educational Leadership* 49, 8: 39–40.

Peck, K., and D. Dorricott. (1994). "Why Use Technology?" *Educational Leadership* 15, 7: 11–14.

Perrone, V. (1991). *Expanding Student Assessment.* Alexandria, Va.: Association for Supervision and Curriculum Development.

Perrone, V. (1994). "How to Engage Students in Learning." *Educational Leadership* 51, 5: 11–13.

Peterson, M., B. LeRoy, S. Field, and P. Wood. (1992). "Community-Referenced Learning in Inclusive Schools: Effective Curriculum for All Students." In *Curriculum Considerations in Inclusive Classrooms: Facilitating Learning for All* (pp. 207–227), edited by S. Stainback and W. Stainback. Baltimore: Paul H. Brookes.

Peterson, P., E. Fennema, and T. Carpenter. (1988–1989). "Using Knowledge of How Students Think About Math." *Educational Leadership* 46, 4: 42–46.

Peterson, P., and N. Knapp. (1993). "Inventing and Reinventing Ideas: Constructivist Teaching and Learning in Mathematics." In *Challenges and Achievements of American Education*, edited by G. Cawelti. 1993 ASCD Yearbook. Alexandria, Va.: Association for Supervision and Curriculum Development.

Poplin, M.S., and S. Stone. (1992). "Paradigm Shifts in Instructional Strategies: From Reductionism to Holistic/Constructivism." In *Controversial Issues Confronting Special Education: Divergent Perspectives*, edited by W. Stainback and S. Stainback. Boston: Allyn and Bacon.

Resnick, L.B., and L.E. Klopfer. (1989). *Toward the Thinking Curriculum: Current Cognitive Research*. Alexandria, Va.: Association for Supervision and Curriculum Development.

Sapon-Shevin, M., B.J. Ayres, and J. Duncan. (1994). "Cooperative Learning and Inclusion." In *Creativity and Collaborative Learning: A Practical Guide to Empowering Students and Teachers*, edited by J. Thousand, R. Villa, and A. Nevin. Baltimore: Paul H. Brookes.

Schrumpf, F. (1994). "The Role of Students in Resolving Conflicts in Schools." In *Creativity and Collaborative Learning: A Practical Guide to Empowering Students and Teachers*, edited by J. Thousand, R. Villa, and A. Nevin. Baltimore: Paul H. Brookes.

Shriner, J.G., J.E. Ysseldyke, M.L. Thurlow, and D. Honetschlager. (1994). "'All' Means 'All': Including Students with Disabilities." *Educational Leadership* 51, 6: 38–42.

Siegel, J., and M. Shaughnessy. (March 1994). "An Interview with Howard Gardner: Educating for Understanding." *Phi Delta Kappan* 75, 7: 563–566.

Sleeter, C., and C. Grant. (1994). "Education That Is Multicultural and Social Reconstructionist." In *Making Choices for Multicultural Education: Five Approaches to Race, Class, and Gender* (2nd ed.), edited by C. Sleeter and C. Grant. New York: Merrill.

Spady, W., and K. Marshall. (1991). "Beyond Traditional Outcome-Based Education." *Educational Leadership* 49, 2: 67–72.

Thornburg, D. (1992). *Edutrends 2010*. San Carlos, Calif.: Starsong Publications.

Thousand, J., R. Villa, and A. Nevin. (1994). *Creativity and Collaborative Learning: A Practical Guide to Empowering Students and Teachers.* Baltimore: Paul H. Brookes.

Tiedt, P., and I. Tiedt. (1990). "Education for Multicultural Understanding." In *Multicultural Teaching: A Handbook of Activities, Information, and Resources* (3rd ed.), edited by P. Tiedt and I. Tiedt. Boston: Allyn and Bacon.

Vermont State Department of Education. (1993). *Vermont's Common Core of Learning: The Results We Need from Education.* Montpelier, Vt.: Vermont State Department of Education.

Villa, R., and J. Thousand. (1992). "Student Collaboration: An Essential for Curriculum Delivery in the 21st Century." In *Curriculum Considerations in Inclusive Classrooms: Facilitating Learning for All Students,* edited by S. Stainback and W. Stainback. Baltimore: Paul H. Brookes.

Villa, R., J. Udis, and J. Thousand. (1994). "Responses for Children Experiencing Behavioral and Emotional Challenges." In *Creativity and Collaborative Learning: A Practical Guide to Empowering Students and Teachers,* edited by J. Thousand, R. Villa, and A. Nevin. Baltimore: Paul H. Brookes.

Wiggins, G. (1989). "Teaching to the (Authentic) Test." *Educational Leadership* 46, 7: 41–47.

Zessoules, R., and H. Gardner. (1991). "Authentic Assessment: Beyond the Buzzword and Into the Classroom." In *Expanding Student Assessment,* edited by V. Perrone. Alexandria, Va.: Association for Supervision and Curriculum Development.

6

A Process for Adapting Curriculum in Inclusive Classrooms

Alice Udvari-Solner

> Doing better at the same old thing isn't good enough. The idea
> is not to fix things, it is to change them. (Walsh as cited in
> Maulson 1991, p. 49)

This statement by a Chicago public school teacher embodies the spirit
of innovation and conceptual change needed to respond to the needs
of an increasingly diverse student population while fostering the educational goals of belonging, mastery, independence, and generosity,
which were articulated in Chapter 3. The movement toward inclusion
is a sociopolitical process (Wisniewski and Alper 1994) that not only
requires shared values about students and learning but also significant
innovation and adaptation in instructional practices.

In that regard, teachers have been viewed simultaneously in two ways: as agents of innovation due to their intimate, day-to-day interaction with issues of diversity and as major hindrances to change because of their reliance on outdated or traditional modes of instruction (Prawat 1990). This chapter describes the form and function of successful curriculum adaptations and a process for decision making when such adaptations are needed. This process is a result of working with general and special educators as they attempted to include students with disabilities (Udvari-Solner 1995).

Form and Function of Curricular Adaptations

Curricular adaptations are modifications that relate specifically to instruction or curriculum content in general education environments. A curricular adaptation is any adjustment or modification in the environment, instruction, or materials used for learning that enhances a person's performance or allows at least partial participation in an activity (Baumgart, Brown, Pumpian, Nisbet, Ford, Sweet, Messina, and Schroeder 1982; Udvari-Solner 1992).

An adaptation identified as "effective" by teachers, parents, paraprofessionals, therapists, and students themselves fulfills one or more of the following functions:

• It assists the individual to compensate for intellectual, physical, sensory, or behavioral challenges (Nisbet, Sweet, Ford, Shiraga, Udvari, York, Messina, and Schroeder 1983).

• It allows the individual to use current skills while promoting the acquisition of new ones.

• It prevents a mismatch between the student's skills and the general education lesson content (Giangreco and Putnam 1991).

• It reduces the level of abstract information to make content relevant to the student's current and future life.

• It creates a match between the student's learning style and the instructor's teaching style.

Formulating and understanding the purpose of the adaptation in relationship to the learning needs of the students is an essential step in the design and selection process.

A Decision-Making Process

Teachers who successfully include students with diverse learning characteristics constantly make decisions about what will be adapted, adjusted, reconfigured, streamlined, and clarified in their curriculum and instruction. Figure 6.1 outlines a decision-making process that was formulated to conceptualize the acts of selecting and using curricular adaptations.

When a student with disabilities is included in general education, team members routinely discuss several points as an essential first step toward effective programming. They identify and discuss the student's individual educational goals and objectives that will be emphasized across general education settings and activities. Concurrently, they create a picture of the student as a learner and articulate performance expectations. Dialogue on these points helps establish a shared vision for the student's active involvement and guards against discrepant or unrealistic expectations by any team member. This team discourse establishes familiarity with the student, an understanding of the general education program and setting, and a basic schedule of the student's participation throughout the school day and week.

Some teams carry out this exchange informally, simply by talking about the student's preferences and learning style, past instructional methods, and the current individual education program. Others develop more formal communication tools to expedite and ensure understanding among team members. In their extensive work with educators, Giangreco, Cloninger, and Iverson (1993) and Thousand and Villa (1993) promote the use of two communication tools that have been particularly effective in helping teachers document student information: the Program-at-a-Glance and the Individual Education Program (IEP)/ General Education Matrix.

The Program-at-a-Glance provides a medium to summarize the student's primary objectives, generate a brief positive profile of the student, and identify any critical management needs (i.e., mobility, repositioning, eating, toileting, or behavioral issues). The IEP/General Education Matrix extends this information by interfacing the student's IEP goals with the daily activities and schedule of general education environments. This format helps the team make decisions about where and when a student's objectives will best be met and implemented.

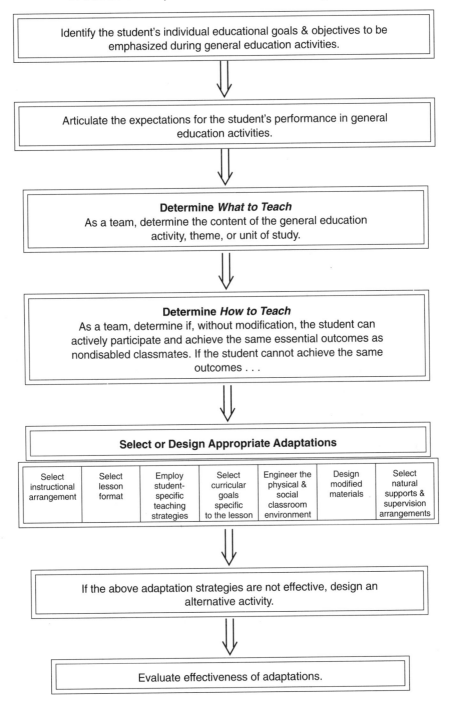

FIGURE 6.1
A Curricular Adaptation and Decision-Making Process

Identify the student's individual educational goals & objectives to be emphasized during general education activities.

Articulate the expectations for the student's performance in general education activities.

Determine *What to Teach*
As a team, determine the content of the general education activity, theme, or unit of study.

Determine *How to Teach*
As a team, determine if, without modification, the student can actively participate and achieve the same essential outcomes as nondisabled classmates. If the student cannot achieve the same outcomes . . .

Select or Design Appropriate Adaptations

| Select instructional arrangement | Select lesson format | Employ student-specific teaching strategies | Select curricular goals specific to the lesson | Engineer the physical & social classroom environment | Design modified materials | Select natural supports & supervision arrangements |

If the above adaptation strategies are not effective, design an alternative activity.

Evaluate effectiveness of adaptations.

Figures 6.2 and 6.3 show a completed Program-at-a-Glance and IEP/General Education Matrix for a 3rd grade student with severe disabilities.

The process of selecting or designing appropriate adaptations is presented through the following series of questions. The adaptation strategies embedded in this process progress from the least to most intrusive means of modification. In this way, teachers first consider

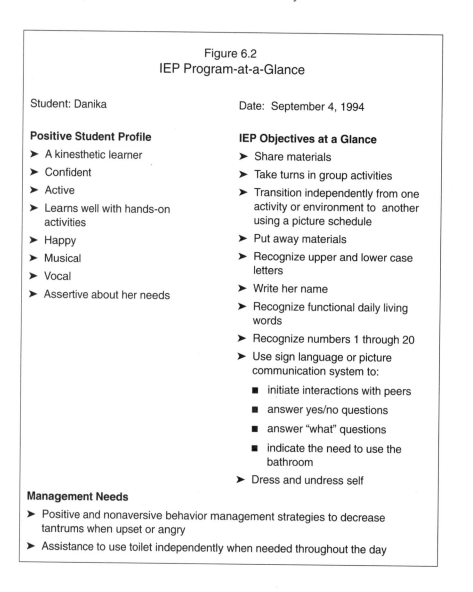

Figure 6.2
IEP Program-at-a-Glance

Student: Danika   Date: September 4, 1994

Positive Student Profile

➤ A kinesthetic learner

➤ Confident

➤ Active

➤ Learns well with hands-on activities

➤ Happy

➤ Musical

➤ Vocal

➤ Assertive about her needs

IEP Objectives at a Glance

➤ Share materials

➤ Take turns in group activities

➤ Transition independently from one activity or environment to another using a picture schedule

➤ Put away materials

➤ Recognize upper and lower case letters

➤ Write her name

➤ Recognize functional daily living words

➤ Recognize numbers 1 through 20

➤ Use sign language or picture communication system to:

■ initiate interactions with peers

■ answer yes/no questions

■ answer "what" questions

■ indicate the need to use the bathroom

➤ Dress and undress self

Management Needs

➤ Positive and nonaversive behavior management strategies to decrease tantrums when upset or angry

➤ Assistance to use toilet independently when needed throughout the day

FIGURE 6.3
Individual Educational Program (IEP)/General Education Matrix

Student: Danika

Date: September 4, 1994

IEP Goals	General Education Class Schedule										
	Arrival/ Schedule	Language Arts	Soc.St./ Science	Art	Music	Phys. Ed.	Lunch	Recess	Journal Writing	Math	Computer Lab
Share materials		✓	✓	✓	✓	✓		✓			✓
Take turns in group activities		✓	✓	✓	✓	✓		✓		✓	✓
Transition between activities/ environments	✓	✓	✓	✓	✓	✓	✓	✓	✓	✓	✓
Put away materials	✓	✓	✓	✓	✓	✓	✓		✓	✓	✓
Recognize upper & lower case letters	✓	✓	✓	✓	✓				✓	✓	✓
Write her name		✓	✓	✓					✓	✓	✓
Recognize/use functional daily living words	✓	✓	✓						✓		✓
Initiate interactions with peers*	✓	✓	✓	✓	✓	✓	✓	✓	✓	✓	✓
Request a partner for play or work*		✓	✓	✓		✓	✓	✓	✓		✓
Answer yes/no questions*	✓	✓	✓	✓	✓	✓	✓	✓	✓	✓	✓
Answer "what" questions*	✓	✓	✓	✓	✓	✓	✓	✓	✓	✓	✓
Indicate the need to use the bathroom*	✓					✓		✓			
Dress and undress self						✓		✓			
Recognize numbers 1 through 20	✓		✓		✓	✓				✓	✓
Management Needs											
Managing anger and reducing tantrums	✓	✓	✓	✓	✓	✓	✓	✓	✓	✓	✓
Assistance with toileting	✓					✓	✓	✓			

*Using sign language or picture communication system.

changes in the essential elements of lesson design before imposing more complex and potentially stigmatizing adaptations.

Can the student actively participate in the lesson without modifications, and will the same essential outcome be achieved?

At many points in the day or week, adaptations will not be needed. Teams should identify these times, feel good about them, and save their energy to address lessons that need significant alterations. Just as there is danger in not providing sufficient adaptations, there is danger in overadapting or oversupporting a student when it is unneeded. As a guideline, determine if the student with disabilities will achieve or experience the same essential outcome as peers without disabilities if there is no modification. If not, supplementary adaptations are most likely warranted.

Can the student's participation be increased by changing the instructional arrangement?

Teachers can choose from a number of instructional arrangements to structure any given subject or lesson. The most common alternatives for student groupings include: large-group or whole-class instruction, teacher-directed small-group instruction, small-group learning, one-to-one teacher/student instruction, independent seat work, partner learning, peer or cross-age tutors, and cooperative learning groups. Such instructional arrangements can have profound effects on how lessons are taught and how students are expected or allowed to participate.

The instructional groupings of choice in most American classrooms continue to be whole class and independent seat work—arrangements that often pose problems for students with disabilities. Departing from traditional instructional arrangements and employing small-group or peer-mediated learning may be one of the most effective steps toward facilitating the inclusion of a student with disabilities. Teacher-directed groups and small-group learning allow more opportunities for teacher/student and student/student contact than either large group or independent seat work. The use of peer-mediated learning including cooperative groups and peer or cross-age tutoring provides frequent opportunities to build social skill repertoires, improve active participation, promote student initiation, and apply skills contextually (Davidson 1994; Harper, Maheady, and Mallette 1994).

Can the student's participation be increased by changing the lesson format?

Lesson format refers to the organizational anatomy of an activity that influences how information is imparted to the student and how the student takes part in learning. The traditional and most frequently used lesson format is the expository mode of teaching, also known as lecture/demonstration/practice (Callahan and Clark 1988). In this format, the teacher is often referred to as "the teller," providing an explanation of a concept or topic, then supporting verbal information with an illustration or model. Typically, students participate in a class discussion or practice the concepts following the teacher's lecture/demonstration. Unfortunately, many teachers and students, particularly at the secondary level, have come to believe that teaching is synonymous with lecturing (Novak 1986). This traditional teaching paradigm is commonly textbook driven and employs a teach-practice-test methodology.

In keeping with best practices of classroom organization, teachers must consider the use of thematic, activity-based, experiential, and community-referenced lesson formats to facilitate the participation of students with disabilities. These formats are generative by reinforcing or extending the lesson content and encouraging students to apply information that has been previously taught or discussed. Plainly, students *do* something that helps illuminate the concept or skill. Learning takes place as a dynamic interaction between the student and the environment (Sharan and Sharan 1976). Characteristics common to all of these formats are that students are actively engaged, participate in the planning process and help define the content (Perrone 1994), learn by discovery, and construct their own knowledge.

Can the student's participation and understanding be increased by changing the delivery of instruction or teaching style?

As stated previously, one of the essential functions of an adaptation is to create a match between the student's learning style and the teacher's teaching style. Frank Smith (1986) relates the importance of teacher behavior:

> Teachers are effective when they make themselves understandable to the learner, no matter how little the learner knows, not when they overwhelm the learner in vain hope that understanding will eventually follow. It is the teacher's responsibility to be comprehensible, not the student's to comprehend (p. 42).

The general educator's teaching style or instructional delivery directly affects the need a student with disabilities may have for supplementary assistance (for example, support facilitators or paraprofessionals). The teacher's words, cues, prompts, checks for understanding, corrective feedback, questioning procedures, physical guidance, and pacing or sequence of instruction are included in the broad definition of teaching style (Salend 1994).

The best-designed adaptations in the form of instructional arrangements, lesson formats, and materials may be in place—but students with disabilities are often destined to fail if the general education teacher does not interact proactively and take instructional responsibility.

The decision to alter teaching style requires the most personal reflection by those who instruct the student. In my experience, when educators view changes in the delivery of their instruction as a legitimate form of adaptation and openly discuss the potential impact of instructional style, they usually generate effective, student-specific teaching strategies.

Will the student need adapted curricular goals?

In a classroom of heterogeneous learners, students will acquire knowledge at different levels and use that knowledge with varying degrees of proficiency (Bloom 1956). Consequently, students' learning priorities will vary in complexity, depth, and breadth. Specifying multilevel or flexible learning objectives (Giangreco and Putnam 1991; Stainback, Stainback, and Moravec 1992) is necessary to individualize the goals and outcomes of the lesson for many students. Prescribing curricular goals and outcomes before each lesson can help ensure that educators establish reasonable expectations while at the same time arrange learning that challenges the student. Establishing curricular goals as they relate to new activities also prompts the team to revisit the student's broader individual educational goals and objectives.

Curricular goals can be modified to:

• relate to the same content but be less complex;
• have functional or direct applications;
• reduce the performance standards;
• adjust the pacing of a lesson (e.g., the student may require more or less time to complete a task);
• adjust the evaluation criteria or grading system; and
• alter behavior management techniques. (For a more detailed discussion of alternative evaluation systems, see Cullen and Pratt 1992 and Udvari-Solner 1994.)

Consider the following example of journal writing in a 3rd grade classroom. The curricular goal for the majority of students is to preface their journal entries with their name and the date, then write a brief paragraph to summarize their thoughts and feelings about the day. These goals reflect skills requiring application, analysis, and synthesis.

Justin, a member of the class with moderate intellectual and physical disabilities, uses picture symbols for communication, is unable to write, and does not construct complex sentences. His goals are to use a date and name stamp to preface his journal entry, select one picture symbol and glue it into his journal to represent an activity that occurred during the day, and use his journal entry to initiate a conversation with a class-mate. Justin's goals represent learning at his knowledge and compre-hension levels. His goals relate to the same content (journal writing) but are less complex. Performance standards also have been varied to cor-respond with and advance Justin's primary mode of communication.

Can changes be made in the classroom environment or lesson location that will facilitate participation?

From a social-ecological perspective, the physical environment and social climate of a classroom influences the behavior and interactions of its members (Moos 1979). Circumstances in the learning environment can affect any student's ability to acquire information. Upon entering an environment, individuals attempt to adapt or adjust to a physical setting, the people around them, and the social milieu. However, some students may be less able to establish personal congruence with the pre-existing conditions of a classroom or school setting (Moos and Trickett 1979). For these students, the physical and social environment may need to be engineered consciously. Environmental elements such as lighting, noise level, visual and auditory input, physical arrangement of the room or equipment, and accessibility of materials may need to be altered to accommodate students with sensory impairments, physical disabilities, information-processing difficulties, or alternative commu-nication methods (Casella and Bigge 1988).

Making changes in the social climate or social rules of the classroom can have powerful effects on the satisfaction, comfort level, and per-sonal growth of a student with disabilities. Modifications in social rules may relate to time allowed to converse and socialize in the classroom, the noise level typically tolerated during work periods, or the flexibility to move about in the classroom during instruction. Teachers must consider the explicit and implicit social rules they have constructed in their classrooms and determine if any elements require change to promote a better student/environment match.

Will different instructional materials be needed to ensure participation?

Instructional materials are the medium through which teachers present essential concepts and constructs. They are also the means by which students access information and demonstrate their comprehension and understanding. The traditional artifacts of teaching—textbooks, worksheets, paper and pencils—offer a narrow range of access and expression. The more varied and rich the materials, the more avenues for expression and opportunities to capture evidence of the student's knowledge.

Students with disabilities may use the same materials as other students in class, require slight variations, or need alternative materials. Materials may be changed or created to be more easily manipulated, concrete, tangible, contextually based, simplified, and matched to the student's learning style or comprehension level. When variations in materials are made, team members should evaluate the products to ensure that they remain age appropriate and status enhancing.

Changes in materials can allow a different mode of output by the student or allow a different mode of input to the student. Consider the following example. In a 9th grade drama class, students are expected to perform a dialogue with a peer partner using an excerpt from a screenplay. Paul is a student with Down syndrome who reads at approximately the 1st grade level. To take part in this activity, Paul's peer partner modifies the screenplay by rewriting his part in simplified and common language. Picture symbols are added for clarification. Paul's partner also records the modified dialogue on an audiotape so Paul can review and practice using auditory input, thereby guiding his pacing and voice intonation.

As part of the requirement for the class, all dialogue partners are expected to modify their screenplays in some fashion. Some students change the gender or professions of the characters. Others may take a screenplay written in the 1950s and update it with contemporary language and social issues. Because the expectation to change materials is applied to all class members, variations for Paul are not considered unusual, stigmatizing, or unreasonable. The adaptations developed for Paul represent variation in form and complexity and provide a different mode of input. This example also illustrates how adaptations can be infused into daily classroom operations and student assignments.

Will personal assistance be needed to ensure participation?

To facilitate inclusion and independence, an implicit goal should be to reduce a student's need for paid or specialized assistance over time. It is true that some students with disabilities need higher levels of assistance or intervention than are provided to typical students. Support needs may vary day to day or be required at predictable times. Rarely do students need continuous, ongoing supervision. Thus, assistance and instruction from someone outside of the classroom structure should be flexible and determined by the student's need within a particular setting or lesson. It is preferable to use natural supports or support by the general education teacher and peers to the greatest extent possible. Unfortunately, the assignment of additional human support to a classroom is frequently made at the beginning of the school year and more often is based on the general educator's desire for additional help than a student's true need for assistance.

Permanent, full-time assistance within a classroom must be assigned cautiously. When there are no concerted plans to phase out the level and intensity of outside support, few efforts are made to facilitate the general educator's ownership of the student with unique learning needs. The type of support needed for the student to meaningfully participate—and whether that support can be provided as an unobtrusive part of the general educator's current instructional routine—must be considered as lessons are designed. When additional support is warranted, a variety of members in the school community—including peers, cross-age tutors, related service personnel, and classroom volunteers—may serve as viable instructional agents (Thousand, Villa, and Nevin 1994; Vandercook and York 1990; York, Giangreco, Vandercook, and MacDonald 1992).

Will an alternative activity need to be designed for the student and a small group of peers?

An alternative activity can be employed when changes outlined in the previous questions are insufficient. By design, such an activity would include the student with disabilities and a partner or a small group of nondisabled peers (Udvari-Solner 1992). Merely arranging one-to-one instruction with an instructional assistant in the same room does not constitute an alternative activity. An alternative activity is:

• often activity-based or experiential in nature and in some instances may be community referenced,
   • similar or related to the curriculum content of the class, and
   • meaningful and age appropriate for all students involved.

When teachers employ alternative activities, they commit to allowing more than one task to take place within the classroom or to allowing
activities to take place outside the classroom. As one example, a 7th
grade language arts teacher used schoolwide survey teams as an alternative activity. Each week the class selected a question related to the
course content or an issue of importance to the school community.
Equipped with "the question of the week," a small survey team including a student with disabilities was assigned to poll a representative
number of the student body. The survey team was arranged in a
cooperative format allowing roles for an interviewer, transcriber, and
data analyzer. This ongoing and readily available activity allowed the
student with disabilities and his classmates to apply various language
and communication skills.

℘ ℘ ℘

Introducing innovation into classroom practice is a highly personal
and often emotionally charged experience. Change may be positively
promoted by supporting teachers to engage in reflective action—the
active, thoughtful, and rigorous consideration of beliefs and practice
(Dewey 1933). There appears to be value in providing teachers with an
initial framework for decision making to initiate reflective action, aid
development, and prompt use of existing knowledge in new configu-
rations for *all* students.

References

Baumgart, D., L. Brown, I. Pumpian, J. Nisbet, A. Ford, M. Sweet, R. Messina,
    and J. Schroeder. (1982). "Principle of Partial Participation and Individual-
    ized Adaptations in Educational Programs for Severely Handicapped Stu-
    dents." *The Journal for Persons with Severe Handicaps* 7: 17–43.
Bloom, B.S. (1956). *Taxonomy of Educational Objectives: Handbook I. Cognitive
    Domain.* New York: David McCay Co.
Callahan, J., and L. Clark. (1988). *Teaching in the Middle and Secondary Schools:
    Planning for Competence (3rd ed.).* New York: MacMillan Publishing.

Casella, V., and J. Bigge. (1988). "Modifying Instructional Modalities and Conditions for Curriculum Access." In *Curriculum-Based Instruction for Special Education Students,* edited by J. Bigge. Mountain View, Calif.: Mayfield Publishing Company.

Cullen, B., and T. Pratt. (1992). "Measuring and Reporting Student Progress." In *Curriculum Considerations in Inclusive Classrooms: Facilitating Learning for All Students,* edited by S. Stainback and B. Stainback. Baltimore: Paul H. Brookes.

Davidson, N. (1994). "Cooperative and Collaborative Learning: An Integrated Perspective." In *Creativity and Collaborative Learning: A Practical Guide to Empowering Students and Teachers,* edited by J. Thousand, R. Villa, and A. Nevin. Baltimore: Paul H. Brookes.

Dewey, J. (1933). *How We Think: A Restatement of the Relation of Reflective Thinking to the Education Process.* Chicago: Henry Regnery and Co.

Giangreco, M., C. Cloninger, and V. Iverson. (1993). *Choosing Options and Accommodations for Children (COACH): A Guide to Planning Inclusive Education.* Baltimore: Paul H. Brookes.

Giangreco, M., and J. Putnam. (1991). "Supporting the Education of Students with Severe Disabilities in Regular Education Environments." In *Critical Issues in the Lives of People with Severe Disabilities,* edited by L. Meyer, C. Peck, and L. Brown. Baltimore: Paul H. Brookes.

Harper, G.F., L. Maheady, and B. Mallette. (1994). "The Power of Peer-Mediated Instruction: How and Why It Promotes Academic Success for All Students." In *Creativity and Collaborative Learning: A Practical Guide to Empowering Students and Teachers,* edited by J. Thousand, R. Villa, and A. Nevin. Baltimore: Paul H. Brookes.

Maulson, T. (February 1991). "Heros and Heroines." *Mother Jones,* pp. 42–51.

Moos, R. (1979). *Evaluating Educational Environments.* San Francisco: Jossey-Bass.

Moos, R., and E. Trickett. (1979). "Architectural, Organizational, and Contextual Influences on Classroom Learning Environments." In *Evaluating Educational Environments,* edited by R. Moos. San Francisco: Jossey-Bass.

Nisbet, J., M. Sweet, A. Ford, B. Shiraga, A. Udvari, J. York, R. Messina, and J. Schroeder. (1983). "Utilizing Adaptive Devices with Severely Handicapped Students." In *Educational Programs for Severely Handicapped Students, Vol XIII,* edited by L. Brown, A. Ford, J. Nisbet, M. Sweet, B. Shiraga, J. York, R. Loomis, and P. VanDeventer. Madison, Wisc.: Madison Metropolitan School District.

Novak, J. (1986). *A Theory of Education.* Ithaca, N.Y.: Cornell University Press.

Perrone, V. (February 1994). "How to Engage Students in Learning." *Educational Leadership* 51, 5: 11–13.

Prawat, R. (1990). *Changing Schools by Changing Teachers' Beliefs about Teaching and Learning. (Elementary Subjects Center Series No. 19).* Lansing, Mich.:

Michigan State University, Center for the Learning and Teaching of Elementary Subjects Institute for Research on Teaching.

Salend, S. (1994). *Effective Mainstreaming: Creating Inclusive Classrooms.* New York: Macmillan Publishing Co.

Sharan, S., and Y. Sharan. (1976). *Small Group Teaching.* Englewood Cliffs, N.J.: Educational Technology Publications.

Smith, F. (1986). *Insult to Intelligence: The Bureaucratic Invasion of our Classrooms.* New York: Arbor House.

Stainback, S., W. Stainback, and J. Moravec. (1992). "Using Curriculum to Build Inclusive Classrooms." In *Curriculum Considerations in Inclusive Classrooms; Facilitating Learning for all Students,* edited by S. Stainback and W. Stainback. Baltimore: Paul H. Brookes.

Thousand, J., and R. Villa. (1993). "Strategies for Educating Learners with Severe Handicaps Within Their Local Home Schools and Communities." In *Challenges Facing Special Education,* edited by E.L. Meyen, G.A. Vergason, and R.J. Whelan. Denver: Love Publishing.

Thousand, J., R. Villa, and A. Nevin. (1994). *Creativity and Collaborative Learning: A Practical Guide to Empowering Students and Teachers.* Baltimore: Paul H. Brookes.

Udvari-Solner, A. (1992). *Curricular Adaptations: Accommodating the Instructional Needs of Diverse Learners in the Context of General Education.* Monograph. Kansas State Board of Education—Services for Children and Youth with Deaf-Blindness Project.

Udvari-Solner, A. (1994). "A Decision-Making Model for the Use of Curricular Adaptations in Cooperative Groups." In *Creativity and Collaboration: A Practical Guide to Empowering Students and Teachers,* edited by J. Thousand, R. Villa, and A. Nevins. Baltimore: Paul H. Brookes.

Udvari-Solner, A. (1995). "Examining Teacher Thinking: Constructing a Process to Design Curricular Adaptations." Manuscript submitted for publication.

Vandercook, T., and J. York. (1990). "A Team Approach to Program Development and Support." In *Support Networks for Inclusive Schooling: Interdependent Integrated Education,* edited by W. Stainback and S. Stainback. Baltimore: Paul H. Brookes.

Wisniewski, L., and S. Alper. (1994). "Including Students with Severe Disabilities in General Education Settings." *Remedial and Special Education* 7, 2: 49–53.

York, J., M. Giangreco, T. Vandercook, and C. Macdonald. (1992). "Integrating Support Personnel in the Inclusive Classroom." In *Curriculum Considerations in Inclusive Classrooms: Facilitating Learning for all Students,* edited by S. Stainback and W. Stainback. Baltimore: Paul H. Brookes.

Voice of Inclusion: Everything About Bob Was Cool, Including the Cookies

Richard A. Villa

" I made Bob a promise. Now, I know that I won't be able to keep it. I feel really bad about that. I don't know if I can tell you about it. I don't know if I should." These were words spoken to me by a student named Bubba. Who is Bubba? Who is Bob? What was the promise, and why couldn't Bubba keep it?

Bob Comes to Winooski

I first heard about Bob in November of 1987. Totyona, a woman who had once worked in the Winooski, Vermont, School District, called me on the phone to ask if a foster child who was to come and live with her could go to school in Winooski. Since Totyona and her husband, Todd, both resided in Winooski, my answer, of course, was yes.

Bob was a young man with multiple disabilities. For 14 years, he had lived with his parents in a small town in northeastern Vermont. Totyona met him when he attended her special education class. In May of 1987, when Bob's mom become ill and was no longer able to care for him, Bob went to live in a residential medical educational facility. His initial stay was to have been six weeks. By the time Totyona called me, he had been there six months. With Bob's mom still unable to care for him, his stay had been extended. Although Bob was not able to communicate orally or through sign language, other devices, or the consistent use of smiles or frowns, I believe he did communicate his sense of loss during the time he was at the residential facility: His weight dropped by 16 pounds.

Bob was the first student with severe disabilities to be integrated into the mainstream of the Winooski School District. A great deal of planning went into Bob's transition, and his natural parents and foster mother were all part of the initial transition meetings. We met with everyone at the residential facility that provided services to Bob. We observed and videotaped Bob. A team of general and special educators from Winooski visited the facility. We then detailed a plan for his transition. Our goal was for Bob to attend school full time in Winooski within six weeks.

In retrospect, one of the most important transition activities was the immediate involvement of other students. A special educator who became Bob's service coordinator joined me in visiting every junior high classroom and speaking with the students. In a sense, we "introduced" Bob to them. We showed a videotape of Bob and described what we knew about him, including his strengths and some of his needs. Even though we didn't know a great deal about Bob, we pretended to know even less. We asked the students to help us brainstorm strategies and resources to support Bob in his new school.

The response of the students was great. Their advice ranged from the kind of musical tapes and "Trapper Keeper" notebooks Bob should have so that he'd fit in, to where he should hang out to be "cool." In 1987, if you were a junior high school student, the cool place to hang out was by the bike rack. Students asked many questions, including how we intended to grade Bob. It was clear that we would need to make some accommodations.

Laura, a junior high school student who also happened to be the daughter of the superintendent, was one of the students who greatly anticipated Bob's arrival. I learned in a conversation with the superintendent that he had overheard his daughter speak to her friends about Bob's impending arrival with such excitement that he thought Bob was a rock star or teen idol who was coming to town. Even though Bob had not yet been to the school, he was in fact one of the most "popular" students in the junior high. Everyone who had the opportunity to plan for him got to know about him, talked about him, and wanted to get to meet him in person.

Today, a visitor to the school would not be surprised to see a student with severe disabilities as a natural part of the student body. But in 1987, Bob was "different"—at least initially.

Building Bob's Supports

The team of adults who assembled to work with Bob after his arrival put an extraordinary amount of time and energy into planning for Bob. In the beginning, it seemed that there were many more questions than answers. We secured technical assistance from state and local resources. Having Totyona, Bob's foster mother, as a member of Bob's "core" team was extremely valuable. As his former teacher, and now as one of his parents, she brought a dual perspective to Bob's team—a wealth of information, concerns, and ideas no one else had.

To respond to Bob's needs, the adults and students of the school assumed new roles. For instance, the speech and language pathologist found herself among the personnel who fed Bob at lunchtime. This role change allowed her to assess Bob's oral-motor skills, work with him on communication issues, and establish a relationship with him. Bob needed to be repositioned out of his wheelchair and engaged in range-of-motion exercises daily. For this to happen, some professional and paraprofessional staff received training in handling and positioning techniques and range-of-motion activities so they could share this new job function.

Students also took on new roles. Volunteer tutors were recruited and trained to assist in Bob's educational program. A dozen or so classmates came forth to become his peer support network. Peer buddies and a Circle of Friends (Forest and Lusthaus 1989; Falvey, Rosenberg, Forest, and Pearpoint 1994) helped include Bob in the nonacademic aspects of school and social life outside of school. They met Bob at the bus, got him from class to class, and encouraged and facilitated his attendance at after-school activities.

Bob's network was diverse. It included students who were popular, students who were quiet, students with the full range of academic talent or achievement, and students who had siblings with disabilities. Put together, they had lots of different interests and one particular shared one—a concern for Bob.

Initially, Bob's team targeted three priority individualized educational plan (IEP) goal areas. Communication was of highest priority, with objectives to increase his vocalization and visual tracking ability, establish discrimination among things of importance in his environment, respond to his name, explore ways for him to indicate choice, and develop his use of a switch that eventually could be used to activate electronically assisted communication and other devices.

A second goal area was socialization. Bob's team wanted him to be included in a variety of social activities, have spontaneous interactions with peers, and develop relationships.

His health was another priority. He needed to gain back the 16 pounds he had lost and maintain or regain his range of motion. These goals were met during Bob's first year as a Winooski student.

Snapshots of Bob's School Life: Year 1

How were socialization, health, and increased communication objectives integrated into the curriculum and instructional practices of our junior high school? To start, Bob's team used a matrixing procedure (described in Chapter 6) to examine all the possible times, places, classes, and activities within the general education junior high school schedule (e.g., academic classes, nonacademic classes like physical education and art, and Teacher Advisory period) during which Bob's IEP objectives might be directly or incidentally addressed. The team then developed an initial schedule, which in Bob's first year included science, math, physical education, social studies, library, technology education, computer, and Teacher Advisory classes.

Teacher Advisory

During the morning Teacher Advisory period, Bob frequently worked with some students on the use of a panel switch. Hitting the switch would activate a tape recorder. The tape in the tape player was always music that had been chosen by the students with whom Bob was working. They encouraged Bob to use the panel switch; when he did, they were all reinforced by being able to listen to the music they had selected.

Science Class

As a former junior high school science teacher, I took great interest in observing what went on in Bob's science class and discovered that, in many ways, some things never change. For example, one day when I was observing Bob in science, the class was dissecting frogs. The same things occurred as when I had my students perform dissections. Some students really got into the activity; others found it "gross." And some students wiggled frog parts in front of someone else's face, resulting in giggles and screams.

I was fascinated to see Bob's participation. Students were working in cooperative groups of three at lab tables. Each group had a dissecting pan, a frog in the pan, and dissecting tools. I noticed that Bob's lab group, which consisted of Bob and two other students, wasn't using a lab table like the other groups. Instead, the pan and frog were on the lap tray connected to Bob's wheelchair, and Bob's teammates were gathered around the tray doing their work.

There also were a couple of other objects on the lap tray, including the blue cup that Bob used for drinking water and juices. This seemingly had nothing to do with the dissecting activity—but it had a lot to do with Bob's objectives. Occasionally, during the course of the activity, Bob's teammates would ask, "Bob, do you want a drink?" or "Bob, can you look at the blue cup?" Bob's response to the question was recorded by an instructional assistant who sat to the side. The assistant was not directly involved in the activity, but always available to support Bob or any other student, if needed. The students were well aware of Bob's objectives regarding object discrimination and making choices and easily incorporated them into the dissection activity. (See Chapter 6 for a quick and easy way to communicate priority objectives through a Program-at-a-Glance.)

As for increased vocalizing, Bob laughed and squealed as readily as any of the students when a teammate invariably held up a part of the frog and wiggled it in his face. This observation clearly illustrated for me how aptly students included Bob within planned activities, enabling him to address his objectives while working on their own.

Mathematics

Bob also participated in math class. What did Bob and math class have in common? Since visual tracking was one of Bob's communication objectives, we wanted him to increase his ability to follow movement with his eyes. His math teacher happened to have a booming voice and a habit of pacing back and forth. Positioning Bob in such a way that he could see the teacher, we found Bob following the teacher with his eyes. We even began to see his head move. The teacher always used Bob's and other students' names in the word problems with which he started off each class. For example, after studying the relationship of the radius, diameter, and circumference of a circle, an application might be, "Given the radius of the tires on Bob's wheelchair and the distance from this room to the cafeteria, how many revolutions would it take to get Bob from here to the lunchroom?" The students then could measure, compute, and verify their answers by wheeling Bob to the cafeteria. Activities like this allowed us not only to see if Bob recognized his name, but enabled him to meaningfully participate in and contribute to the classroom community.

In the second half of the class, the teacher usually went on to do some whole-group direct instruction or assigned individual seatwork. This was a time when Bob could work on other IEP goals, go to lunch early (because he needed an extended time to eat lunch), or work with a peer tutor or an instructional assistant on alternative objectives outside of the class or in the community.

Social Studies

Bob's social studies teacher typically began class with "Vermont Stories," an activity in which students came to the front of the room and briefly presented some newsworthy happening. Students were encouraged to report about Vermont events, but were free to report national, world, local, or personal stories. On Bob's day to report the news, the instructional assistant wheeled him to the front of the room and explained to the class a new communication experiment she and Bob had been working on. She placed vertically in front of Bob a large piece of plexiglass that had a symbol for "yes" in the upper-right corner and a symbol for "no" in the left. She then asked Bob a question. To reply, he looked at the appropriate symbol (yes or no) to indicated his preference. She repeated this with students asking questions. In the same amount of time it took for any classmate to tell a Vermont Story, the students became knowledgeable of Bob's new communication program and how to encourage him to use the device throughout the day. From my observation of the students' body language, they were much more attentive to Bob's Vermont story than they were to stories presented by other classmates.

Physical Education

Where do most students have their physical development and education needs addressed? In the same place that Bob had his adaptive physical education needs met—the gym. In gym class, Bob was repositioned to do range-of-motion exercises on a gym mat. During the wrestling unit, Bob was joined on the floor by the other students. Bob went outside whenever his classmates were outside during baseball season and was a designated base runner for his team. When his batting partner hit a ball, Bob was wheeled quickly around the bases. I can still hear his laugh as he went from first to second, to third base, and then home.

Year 2: Entrepreneurism and Social Life

Budding Entrepreneurs

By the start of Bob's second (8th grade) year, his family and support team began to discuss what might happen to Bob after high school. As a consequence, work-related goals were included in his IEP. His team came up with the idea of Bob forming a small cookie manufacturing and sales business with three classmates who had an interest in entrepreneurism. The business was named Cota's Cool Cookies—Cota because that was Bob's last name, and Cool because the secret ingredient was cool mint chocolate chips. Bob was the chief executive officer and the head chef. With the use of his panel switch, he turned on the beater that mixed the cookie batter. The other students in the business baked, packaged, and distributed the cookies.

Cota's Cool Cookies was a collaborative enterprise that involved many students in the school. Students in business class set up contracts and maintained the books for the business. Students in the art classes partici-pated in a contest for the design of the product label. Cota's Cool Cookies were sold in the district's schools and in two neighboring school districts during lunch. They also were sold at the National Guard Armory, Winooski City Hall, and a variety of other places in the community. Despite the numerous supplies that had to be purchased, Bob and his business partners turned a profit within a couple of months.

Life Outside School

Bob's involvement with his peers extended beyond the school day. I remember Totyona, his foster mother, saying, "I used to think it would be so great if Bob had some friends coming over after school. Well, they came. Do you have any idea what it's like to have a half dozen junior high kids in your house all day—with all that energy?"

I will never forget the day a teacher came to me and said, "I think Bob's going to be in a fight." I asked for details and she explained, "You see, Bob has been invited to the Halloween dance by a cheerleader, and her ex-boyfriend, who is on the football team, isn't too happy. He says he's going to pound Bob's face. What are we going to do?" We decided to do what we would do for any other student in junior high. We monitored the situation and planned not to intervene unless it was necessary. After all, changing boyfriends and girlfriends is a part of normal adolescent development. As it turned out, Bob did not get into a fight with the football player. He went to the Halloween dance dressed as Beetle Juice and enjoyed doing wheelies on the dance floor with his classmates.

Transitions

Toward the end of Bob's 8th grade year, Totyona notified the school that Bob would be moving with his foster parents to a neighboring town and school district. His support and friendship circles were saddened by the news, as were teachers, the principal, and myself. When Bob first came to Winooski, everyone wondered how he would fit in and if he would be accepted and appreciated for his individuality.

I remember a teacher's initially saying, "Is he just going to sit in the back of my room, drooling, making noises, and disrupting my class?" The same teacher, six months after getting to know Bob, said, "He has had such a powerfully positive influence on the students. Can he please stay in my class another year?" I reminded the teacher of our school's adherence to the principle of "age-appropriate placement." Bob needed to move along the grades with his peers.

Hearing of Bob's impending move, his peer support circle recalled their own involvement in planning for Bob's arrival 18 months before. Aware of the importance of transition planning, they approached me with a request to speak to the staff and students of the school Bob would attend in the fall. They wanted to make sure that the new people in his life knew what Bob could do and how they could support him. Bob's future school was contacted in the spring, and the following October three students visited the school and met with Bob's new classmates and teachers. The impact of their words and advocacy for their friend was evidenced in the following thank you letter.

> Moriah Gosselin and Jason Messick spoke to Bob's afternoon classes. They spoke articulately and with humor and covered many important aspects of Bob's integration at your school. Most important was the regard and fondness for Bob evident in their presentations. They were excellent.
>
> Chandra Duba, who came to school at 7 a.m. to speak with Bob's morning classes, discussed not only Winooski's experiences with Bob but also her own experiences with handicapped siblings.
>
> Although Bob was the focus of their work, the impact of these young people went far beyond Bob. The attitudes and behaviors they modeled were lessons for us all about friendship and mutual respect. What they taught made the way easier for many handicapped students here (K. Lewis, personal communication, November 20, 1989).

Early in December, Winooski students went back to see how Bob was doing. They excitedly reported that he looked great, seemed happy, and had a whole new peer support network. That Saturday I spoke with Bob's foster parents. They expressed happiness with Bob's transition and his emerging new support group.

On Sunday of the same weekend, sitting at the breakfast table with his foster family, Bob suddenly died. He had contracted an undetected pneumonia that was too much for his fragile system to handle.

On Monday, I delivered the news. In all of my years in education, the hardest thing I have had to do was to gather Bob's Winooski classmates and tell them that their friend had died. Because many of the students wanted to go to Bob's funeral, the school arranged for a bus to take staff and students on the two-hour trip to Bob's hometown.

As I sat in that funeral parlor and looked around, any doubts that I might have had about the benefits of inclusive education disappeared forever. I recalled funerals I had attended of other students who had died, students who had been educated apart from their neighborhood peers. Those funerals usually were attended only by the family and other adults. It seemed to me that in many ways their lives had been anonymous. In contrast, this room was filled with children—the very diverse group of Bob's peers who now were mourning the loss of a friend. Bob had not lived an anonymous life. He had died with dignity, respect, and friendship.

After the funeral, the bus ride home was silent. But, then, little by little, students began to tell stories and anecdotes about Bob. One student recalled playing a joke on a substitute teacher when he turned his back by taking Bob in his wheelchair and disappearing. Another student recalled the superintendent's expressing concern about liability because Bob was being wheeled so quickly around the baseball diamond and athletic fields. They said they didn't care if they got into trouble with the superintendent; it was worth it just to hear Bob laugh as he rounded the bases.

Staff members recalled all the planning that had gone into Bob's initial integration into Winooski and how much was learned from the experience that subsequently benefited many other students. We talked about knowing intuitively how to meet Bob's needs. We reflected on how Bob's presence taught students and adults alike to accept and appreciate the difference in others and within themselves. We talked about the future. What if a classmate of Bob become a parent of a child with a severe disability? Would having known Bob and his zest in life make a difference for that parent? Bob's classmates are the employers of the future. When approached with the prospect of hiring somebody like Bob, they might recall all that Bob was capable of doing and choose to employ that person.

It was at that point that Bubba, a star football, baseball, and hockey player, approached me. "Dr. Villa," he said, "I made Bob a promise. Now, I know that I won't be able to keep it. I feel really bad about that. I don't know if I can tell you about it. I don't know if I should." I encouraged Bubba to say what was on his mind, and he finally did. It seems he had promised Bob that when the two of them turned 21, the legal drinking age in Vermont, they were going to go out and get rip roaring drunk together. Clearly, this may not be what we want students to be thinking about. But it is what many students do anticipate. For me, Bubba's confession was symbolic of a fundamental goal of heterogeneous schooling. You see, Bubba did not see Bob as a "disabled person." Bubba saw Bob as a friend. What Bubba dreamed about for the two of them was no different from what he and other teens dreamed and schemed about, and Bob was a part of it all.

Guidance personnel supported Bob's peers to find ways to express their grief. Some students wrote in journals, others spoke with counselors, and others collected money to donate something in Bob's name and memory. Some expressed anger and frustration at those who prevent students like Bob from attending their neighborhood schools. At that time, a unique opportunity for advocacy came along that helped some students deal with their emotions.

Bob's Advocacy Lives On

Shortly after Bob's death, I became aware of Becky Till, a 14-year-old Canadian girl who, like Bob, had cerebral palsy and lived with a foster family (who eventually were able to adopt her). Becky's foster parents wanted her to attend their community's local school rather than the "special" school. Yet, despite four years of advocacy efforts, they had yet to succeed. We made Winooski students aware of this opportunity, and several wrote to the Ministry of Education of Ontario and the school board members of Becky's town to explain why Becky belonged in school.

To mount further pressure, Becky's mother decided to put on a conference in New Market, Ontario. She invited me and other disability rights advocates to speak. I thought my words might be helpful, but I knew it would be much more important for the audience to listen to the words of students. So two of Bob's friends, Bubba and Moriah, traveled to Ontario and articulated their own and their classmates' views as to why Bob and Becky belonged in school. They spoke of the benefits to all students of being educated together. Bubba expressed emotionally, "Nothing hurts more than losing someone you love." The students were strong and moving in their message, as reflected in the Sunday *Toronto Sun* headline, "Bubba tells Becky, fight until you win!"

It has been several years since Bob's death, but the profound impact he had on my life and the lives of others he touched in his short time on earth lives on. He demonstrated for us the value of collaboration, the value of inclusive education, the value of friendship, and the value of saying yes to the unknown. He is fondly remembered.

Everything about Bob was cool, including Cota's Cool Cookies.

References

Falvey, M., R. Rosenberg, M. Forest, and J. Pearpoint. (1994). "Building Connections." In *Creativity and Collaborative Learning*, edited by J. Thousand, R. Villa, and A. Nevins. Baltimore: Paul H. Brookes.

Forest, M., and E. Lusthaus. (1989). "Promoting Educational Equality for All Students: Circles and MAPs." In *Educating All Students in the Mainstream of Regular Education*, edited by S. Stainback, W. Stainback, and M. Forest. Baltimore: Paul H. Brookes.

7

Questions, Concerns, Beliefs, and Practical Advice About Inclusive Education

Richard A. Villa, Emma Van der Klift, Jonathan Udis,
Jacqueline S. Thousand, Ann I. Nevin, Norman Kunc,
and James W. Chapple

This chapter consists of 16 questions and corresponding "answers." The seven of us who collaborated on this risky venture went into it with a healthy sense of our own limitations in taking on such a task. We know that the usefulness of the insights we offer depends heavily on the context into which they are applied—the individual students, families, teachers, schools, and communities involved.

Our responses were formulated during discussions we held at a week-long school restructuring institute in Vermont. Our intention was to examine the 16 questions we had previously identified as "the most commonly asked" regarding inclusion. As we struggled to identify areas of consensus and divergence in our views, we were all struck by how difficult it is to come up with static, "for all time" answers, given the clear fact that times change, thinking changes, and paradigms change, often quite rapidly.

Further complicating our task was the recognition that objections often come concealed as questions. Questions are often a person's way of saying, "I don't think this will work. Prove to me that it will." When questions contain serious objections, they can appear confrontational and cause people to revert to polarized "black and white," "right versus wrong" thinking and responses, which is always a mistake. In answering the following questions, therefore, we reminded each other that every objection has two components—on the surface, a concern; and somewhere below that, a *belief* (Richard Pimentel, personal communication).

When answering the following questions, we have attempted to move through the concern with serious respect, and also to locate and address the underlying belief. We agreed that every concern would be treated as legitimate. We knew, however, that the underlying beliefs might be problematic. After all, we are products of the various societies in which we live, and many unfounded stereotypes and beliefs about people with disabilities have arisen out of popular "wisdom." These beliefs might be based on a lack of information, misinformation, or even myth. A teacher who has never taught a student with a disability, for example, might worry about behavioral issues because of ideas developed in response to media misrepresentation. Another person might worry about "catching" a disability he believes to be infectious. Someone else might believe that people with disabilities are always more fragile than their nondisabled peers. Each of these things might or might not be true with certain individuals in certain circumstances. But, left unquestioned, our beliefs can influence our behavior when relating to people we encounter in our schools and communities, often in negative and exclusionary ways.

We don't pretend to have definitive answers or a corner on what is "politically correct." The following ruminations simply represent our collective "best thinking" as of January 1995. They are part of a dialogue that we hope will be ongoing and include many other voices in the future.

1. Many parents do not believe that the needs of their children can be met in general education classrooms. Currently, parents have some choice in whether their child attends a general education classroom, resource room, special class, or special school. Will inclusion eliminate parental choice?

Conflict often exists between what parents believe is the best educational setting or approach for their child and what a school offers. This conflict is acted out in various arenas other than special education. Parents who want "traditional" teacher-directed, strict, basic instruction are dissatisfied with an "innovative," student-centered, constructivist approach. Some parents object to outcomes-based education. Still others object to cooperative group learning.

In the past, many parents of children with disabilities did not have a choice about supports to be delivered within the local classroom because the supports were only available in separate places such as resource rooms and special classes and schools. In essence, they had less choice than today. Inclusive policies and practices are not intended to eliminate parental and child choice. There will always be private alternatives to participation in public education programs, and some parents will continue to choose placements other than their community schools. Inclusive educational policies and practices simply make it possible for any child's educational placement of first choice to be the local school and community.

Parents' underlying concern is for their child's success. The belief of some parents that their child will not be successful in general education classrooms is grounded in a history of supports and services *not* being brought into the classroom to ensure success. When special and other support services are melded with general education to deliver exemplary instructional and assessment practices that enable a diverse student population to succeed (e.g., cooperative learning, student-directed and constructivist learning approaches, performance-based assessment), families should see less need for separate programs and alternative choices to general education.

Finally, regardless of parental choice, schools still have the legal obligation to ensure that children and youth with disabilities have the opportunity to be educated with children without disabilities to the maximum extent possible.

2. Are there some children for whom placement in a general education classroom will not be appropriate? Are inclusion advocates suggesting that the federal law be changed and the continuum-of-placement model be discarded?

The first part of this question is not the place to begin a discussion of inclusive education. One of the defining characteristics of an inclusive school is a "zero reject" (Lilly 1971) philosophy—that is, the notion that no child will be excluded from general education classrooms because of a characteristic or trait such as gender, race, socioeconomic status, or a differing ability. Thus, when a discussion of inclusive education begins by identifying which *groups* of children (e.g., medically fragile, children presenting behavior challenges) cannot "make it," we miss the point. Albeit largely unintended, the categorical (or individual) exclusion of children causes peers to wonder, "If my school can exclude them, what would cause it to exclude *me*?" Increasingly, educators and others are recognizing that a solid sense of membership and belonging is a *prerequisite* to excellence and quality in education (refer to the "Circle of Courage" in Chapter 3).

Inclusive education involves a commitment to every child, and every child requires different supports for learning. In this context, a "constellation of services" approach (Nevin, Villa, and Thousand 1992, p. 44), in which needed services are brought to the child rather than taking the child to the services, makes more sense than a continuum-of-placement approach, which presumes removal from the learning community for some children. Ideally, inclusive schools offer a range of supports *within* the general education environments.

The question of student placement—what type of learning environment is most likely to result in meaningful learning—and parental choice are closely linked. It is true that for some students with disabilities the "regular" classroom may not be the optimal learning environment. This is also true for some students *not* identified as disabled. Specifically, in 12 or more years of public schooling, it is unlikely that every teacher whom a student encounters will have all of the characteristics (e.g., content mastery, instructional skills, flexibility, warmth, compassion) parents want for their children. The dream is for a "perfect match" every year; the reality is that most of the time the match is satisfactory. The nightmare is a very poor match.

A first step to take, then, when planning for individual student differences is to identify the unique characteristics, skills, strategies, and knowledge each particular student brings to different learning tasks and to identify likely educational mismatches. Based on a student's characteristics and the demands of a task, a constellation of services, supports, resources, and accommodations can be developed and brought *to* the child to remediate the mismatch and help secure achievement of desired outcomes.

The next step is to determine how best to deliver the instruction, supports, and resources. Few instructional procedures, supports, or resources are completely unique to particular settings. With proper training, coaching, resources, collaboration, and creativity, educators can deliver almost any support or resource almost anywhere. So, then, a continuum-of-placement conceptualization of support reflects educational practices of yesteryear (Reynolds 1962, 1977), which were based on an assumption that services are unique to places and that children need to go to those unique places for those services. Fortunately, our technology and competence for responding to individual student differences has mushroomed over the past decades, as evidenced by the growing number of inclusive schools throughout the United States and Canada. As we get better and better at developing educational experiences that support and include all children, the concept of "continuum" will become less and less relevant. In other words, "placement" decisions and determinations about what constitutes a "least restrictive environment" will become moot points as school communities embrace an inclusive educational philosophy and teach children together rather than apart from one another. Segregated placements will fall by the wayside. We need to actualize the constellation-of-services approach by altering the learning environment to motivate and enable children to succeed rather than removing children from that environment.

With all this said, there clearly are students for whom a traditional "12 years of 185 7-hour school days does not constitute the 'magic formula' for learning" (Villa, Udis, and Thousand 1994, p. 385). For example, some children may desire and benefit from experiences and relationships typically nonexistent within the walls of a classroom or school building. A child might participate in an off-campus counseling group (e.g., for children who have been sexually abused) or employment training in a local business. Another child experiencing emotional difficulties might, for a time, need an altered "school day" that starts and ends on a flexible schedule and includes work and community service opportunities. Yet another student might need a shortened day and a mentor relationship with a respected community member during a period of extreme stress. Still others might need year-long support that includes a summer program to facilitate "staying out of trouble" in the community.

In summary and response to the second part of this question, it might, in fact, be helpful to replace the *continuum-of-placement* language in the U.S. federal law with *constellation-of-services* language to help people understand a new way of delivering supports and services.

3. *Many people within the deaf community do not believe that the educational needs of children who are hard of hearing or deaf can best be met in general education classrooms. How do you address their concerns and desire to immerse their children in deaf culture? Don't parents, advocates, and people who are deaf or hard of hearing know what is best?*

Issues concerning the educational placement of students who are deaf or hard of hearing differ significantly from those pertaining to students with physical, mental, learning, and emotional challenges. The fact that vocal language is relatively inaccessible to these students means that we must address different issues when considering their education and meaningful inclusion into the community.

Like all students, children who are deaf use language to build mental constructs, which, in turn, serve as foundations for future learning. Unlike children who can hear, however, children who are deaf learn language visually—in other words, sight comes before sound. As a result, sign language is, by far, the most accessible language to children who have been deaf from birth. Their learning can be seriously jeopardized if the acquisition and mastery of sign language is delayed by oral training. Understandably, the deaf community has been tenacious in stressing that students who are deaf must attend schools where sign language is the primary language of instruction. Failure to do this can compromise students' comprehension and appreciation of the curriculum.

Some school districts have attempted to address these concerns by using pullout instruction, assigning interpreters to classrooms, and teaching sign to all children. Although these strategies appear to address the problem, many adults who are deaf worry that they are not enough. Members of the hearing community, however well-intentioned and enthusiastic in their attempts to grasp American Sign Language (ASL), may not learn enough "sign as a second language" to provide real conversational stimulation to students. Consequently, students who are deaf might be prevented from experiencing the complexity and richness of sign language during instruction and social interactions.

Nevertheless, serious problems exist with the current education system for children who are deaf or hard of hearing. Most of the programs are regional or magnet schools located in only a few places throughout the country. Therefore, children must often live apart from their families to attend these schools. Advocates for inclusion assert that an educational system that forces people to choose between family life and school is seriously problematic. In addition, segregated schooling typically leads to a lifestyle that remains segregated from the community at large.

The question seems to be whether we, as a society, need to resign ourselves to the idea that a segment of our population must live apart. At the very least, we must attempt to discover the bridges that can link the hearing and nonhearing worlds. We also must continue to explore ways schools can restructure so that students with different languages (i.e., oral and sign) can learn as a common community. There is promise here, which is demonstrated in Vermont where 50 percent of families of children who are deaf or hard of hearing have chosen to place their children in regular education classes at their local schools. When families make such a choice, it becomes the job of teachers and administrators to ensure that the choice does not interfere with a child's acquisition and mastery of sign as a first language, if that is the preferred language; that opportunities are available inside and outside of school for children to interact with others who use sign as a first language and otherwise positively identify with deaf culture, if they choose; and that aspects of the deaf culture are brought into the total culture of the school.

We will only be able to find options that meet all the needs of students who are deaf or hard of hearing when we take into account the perceptions and interests of the deaf community. Hearing professionals have long imposed their educational priorities and goals on students who are deaf. The deaf community has resented these intrusions and remains justifiably skeptical of hearing educators. In no other area of education are we perhaps at greater risk of providing simple solutions to complex problems and forgetting Menke's observation that every complex problem has a simple solution that is invariably wrong.

4. The National Learning Disabilities Association (NLDA) has come out in opposition to inclusion. How do you address their belief that inclusion will not work and that if the inclusion of children with learning disabilities had worked in the past, these children would not have failed or been removed as they were?

NLDA advocacy serves a vital function in ensuring personalized, intensive instruction to optimize the learning potential of students with learning disabilities. Advocates of inclusive education are not recommending the return of children with learning disabilities to the same type of classrooms that initially rejected them. Schools have changed and are continuing to restructure to better meet the needs of these and other children for whom the outcomes of special education have been disappointing.

We need to share what is known and unknown about learning disabilities and how to ameliorate its effects on learning. We know already that not all children with learning disabilities learn in the same way; indeed, homogeneity within any category of disability is a myth. Therefore, a child's unique individual characteristics, rather than any label, must be used to determine the instruction and instructional supports necessary to accommodate that child's learning. (Note: Supports may include training of *both* regular and special educators in an accommodation model such as the one offered in Chapter 6.)

Our collective experience and research (e.g., Thousand, Villa, Meyers, and Nevin 1994) have shown that special and general education teachers are more than willing to expand their repertoires and collaborate with others to personalize education for students with learning disabilities. Teachers unwilling to do so should examine a recent court case (Doe et al. v. Withers 1993) settled in West Virginia in which a high school teacher who refused to follow a student's individualized education plan (IEP) was ordered to pay the student $15,000 plus legal expenses for refusing to make accommodations as required under the Individuals with Disabilities Education Act (IDEA).

5. Inclusion advocates appear to be opposed to any type of homogeneous ability grouping. How are the needs of children identified as gifted and talented going to be met in general education classrooms? These children shouldn't be held back in their learning or be expected to teach other children. They are the leaders of tomorrow.

Inclusion advocates are not categorically against homogeneous grouping. They do, however, understand that no two learners are the same and that grouping of any kind should be short term and for specific, focused instruction. Educators are increasingly aware that intelligence is not a unitary ability; nor is it fixed in time. Emerging conceptualizations of intelligence encompass the idea that people possess "multiple intelligences." Articulated and popularized by Howard Gardner (1983, 1993), multiple intelligences theory suggests at least seven types of intelligences and asserts that learning environments must be structured to nurture students' differing intelligences. The label "gifted and talented," then, takes on new meaning and is best thought of broadly (i.e., students who excel in auto mechanics, computer science, art, or interpersonal intelligences all are "gifted") rather than narrowly (i.e., only students who score highly on linguistic tests of intelligence are gifted).

Current gifted and talented education (GATE) programs expressly celebrate and support the talents of a *few* and have perpetuated racial and socioeconomic segregation, as evidenced by the gross underrepresentation of minority and poor Americans in these programs. In contrast, the purpose of inclusive education is to acknowledge *everyone's* gifts and talents and to help all children reach their potential through the educational experiences historically afforded children in GATE programs (e.g., active, constructivist learning; opportunities to do in-depth, prolonged study of an area of special interest; mentorships and other experiences in the community; use of computer and other technology; access to coursework in community colleges, businesses, and universities). These experiences represent good educational practice and should be an integral part of an inclusive classroom and schooling education for all children.

Reciprocally, former GATE students can greatly benefit from instructional strategies used by inclusive educators to respond to student diversity (e.g., peer-mediated instruction such as peer tutoring and cooperative learning). Specifically, peer-mediated teaching arrangements counter the lack of tolerance of others and the individualistic and competitive work styles that some students develop in homogeneous GATE programs. When implemented well, that is, with each student having individualized outcomes and tasks that contribute to a partnership effort, these strategies allow all students to succeed. Students benefit by engaging in higher-order thinking skills as they organize their thoughts and plan how to effectively communicate material and ideas to their partners in learning, while simultaneously developing the interpersonal leadership skills necessary for the cooperative workplace and world (e.g., trust building, communication, problem solving, conflict resolution).

Inclusive schooling does not mean that children with gifts and talents will not receive focused attention in one-on-one or homogeneous group arrangements. On the contrary, both will be options, as needed, for any student. Capitalizing on the multiple intelligences notion of human difference and potential, homogeneous groups could be arranged along any number of dimensions of interest or "intelligence" (e.g., musical preferences, recreational interests). Robert Slavin (1987) offers a caution here that homogeneous "ability" grouping should occur only when grouping measurably reduces student differences for the targeted skill or concept; when teachers closely monitor student progress and change groupings as students progress; and when teachers actually vary their instruction from one group to the next. Slavin urges that students spend the majority of their school week with a heterogeneous peer group that could include multi-aged, nongraded groupings.

In summary, the tenets of inclusive education have caused many educators to reassess the value of segregated GATE programs (Sapon-Shevin 1994). Removing so-called gifted children from regular classrooms is one more way in which we seem to be "aiming for the middle" (wherever that is) in education. Rather than fostering excellence, the siphoning off of "top" learners contributes directly to a process of making "general" education mediocre. *Perhaps* we can develop "the best" computer programmers and "the best" scientists through a gifted and talented ability-grouping approach. However, some argue that what the world needs most at present are more peacemakers and better collaborators. In fact, employers are saying repeatedly that the workers they seek are those able to interact and work well with an increasingly diverse work force. Ability-grouping practices such as segregated GATE programs work directly against this goal, turning out individuals experienced only at working with others like themselves.

6. Are inclusion advocates primarily concerned with socialization? Are academics being sacrificed?

Academics, socialization, social/emotional development, life skills, employability skill development, and recreation are just a few of the areas of concern when planning a child's individualized program. None of these areas, including academics, should be ignored as a potential priority area for a child with an IEP—or any child, for that matter. When it is acknowledged that not every student must have the same objectives during an activity or lesson, any and all of these areas can be addressed. Further, as many states and communities' education goals now articulate, academics are most important as vehicles for enabling children to achieve the vital results of being good communicators, reasoning problem solvers, responsible citizens in a global society, and nurturers of themselves and others (e.g., Vermont Department of Education 1993). Many educational futurists predict these vital results to be the most important skills for negotiating and surviving the forecasted changes of 21st century life.

We may have mistakenly set up an either/or choice between academics and socialization in school—a kind of "curriculum glaucoma." New instructional practices (see Chapter 5) and theories of learning such as constructivism teach us that learning is a constructed process that includes a social interaction component. Children seem to understand this. For example, when the *Arizona Republic* ("No More School, No More Books" 1994) asked schoolchildren to write about what they regretted leaving behind for summer vacation, they wrote about socialization. A 5-year-old girl wrote, "What I will miss most on my summer vacation is my teachers, and I'll miss seeing my friends. . . ." A 10-year-old boy wrote, "I will miss my teachers . . . and my friends and playing basketball."

Academic, social, emotional, and moral development are inextricably intertwined goals of inclusive education. As Ginott (1972) warns in his letter to teachers (see Chapter 3, Figure 3.2), when emphasis on academics excessively overrides attention to the other areas of human development, we risk repeating historical events of intolerance. It should be noted that at the time of the Holocaust experienced by Ginott, Germany was considered the most highly academically educated society that ever existed. Yet, as Ginott's letter cautions, an academic education in no way ensures social or moral sensitivity, competence, or conscience—aims of 21st century education and inclusive schooling.

7. What is a child with severe disabilities going to do in a 9th grade science course?

This question is really asking why a student who has very different objectives from the majority of class members would be included in an activity or class that does not, at first glance, seem to relate to that student's needs. People often don't realize just how rich a general education environment is, particularly for a student with intensive challenges. The variety of people, materials, and activities is endless and provides an ongoing flow of opportunities for communication and human relationship building, incidental learning in areas not yet targeted as priority objectives, and direct instruction in a student's high-priority learning areas.

Key to a student's meaningful participation is creative thinking on the part of the student's support team, which always has at least four options for arranging the student's participation in general education activities. First, a student can do the *same* things as everyone else (e.g., practice songs in music). Second, *multilevel curriculum and instruction* can occur; that is, all students can be involved in a lesson in the same curriculum area, but pursue varying objectives at multiple levels based on their unique needs. For example, in math, students might be applying computation skills at varying levels—some with complex word problems, others with one-digit subtraction problems, and still others with materials that illustrate counting with correspondence. A third option, *curriculum overlapping*, involves students working on the same lesson, but pursuing objectives from different curricular areas. For example, we learned from the voice "Everything About Bob Was Cool, Including the Cookies" how Bob, a teenager with severe disabilities, worked in a cooperative group, with two other students using his lap tray as the team's work space. Most students were dissecting frogs for the purpose of identifying body parts. Bob's objectives came from the curriculum area of communication. One communication program—discrimination of objects, including his blue drinking cup—was simple for Bob's teammates to carry out along with their dissection throughout the activity. Another communication objective—vocalizing in reaction to others and events—was frequently and readily achieved as Bob giggled and vocalized to teammates' wiggling of frog parts in the air. As still a fourth option, *alternative activities* may be added to a child's schedule to allow for community-based or work options or to address management needs (e.g., catheterization in the nurse's office). Alternative activities can also be considered when regular education activities cannot be adapted.

Extreme caution is advised in ruling an activity "impossible to adapt" or the general education classroom as inappropriate for a student with severe disabilities. Experience has taught us that general education can meet most of the needs of children with severe disabilities, given creative thinking and collaboration on the part of the adults and children in the school and greater community. As Chapter 5 highlights, current theories of learning (e.g., multiple intelligences, constructivist learning), teaching practices that make subject matter more relevant and meaningful (e.g., cooperative group learning, project or activity-based learning, community-referenced activities), and authentic alternatives to paper-and-pencil assessment (e.g., artifact collection for portfolios, role playing, demonstration) empower and equip educators to adapt instruction for any student, including those with severe disabilities.

Finally, to make assumptions about an individual based on a classification of disability is dangerous because it can lead to tunnel vision. Specifically, it can blind us to a person's strengths and abilities, causing us to see only the person's disability—a phenomenon Van der Klift and Kunc (1994) describe as "disability spread" (p. 399). Without looking at a student's strengths and abilities, it is easy to limit expectations, "over-accommodate," or ignore ways those strengths and abilities can be used to motivate and support learning.

8. How do we grade students with disabilities? Is it fair to give them an A or a B for doing work that is significantly different from the rest of the class or after we have provided them with accommodations and modifications to the curriculum and instruction?

We recognize that a diploma or a grade in and of itself tells nothing about what a child knows, believes, or can demonstrate because of the tremendous variability within and across schools as to what a grade or diploma represents. Many traditional grading practices and procedures are arbitrary and subjective. For example, within a particular school, an earned grade in one math class may not mean what the same grade does in another math class (e.g., calculus vs. general math, one trigonometry class vs. another). In fact, within the same class the learning of two students receiving the same grade can be vastly different.

The "correct" approach to student assessment is a hotly debated issue. Some advocate the continuation of competitive, normative comparison practices (i.e., A, B, C, D, and F; percentile scores). Others advocate the adoption of outcomes-based assessment and instructional strategies. The National Center on Education Outcomes, for instance, calls for the identification of outcomes and acceptable performance standards for *all* students, assessment of students with reasonable accommodations if necessary, and the reporting of progress of schools in meeting their stated outcomes (Shriner, Ysseldyke, Thurlow, and Honetschlager 1994).

Performance-based and other authentic assessment approaches are more compatible and supportive of children with and without disabilities than traditional standardized achievement testing. They give those who wish to know about student performance a much richer picture of what students actually can do and the supports they need to do it than standardized tests scores. And is that not what we truly want to know? As Nel Noddings (1992) put it, "We should move away from the question, 'Has Johnny learned X?' to the far more pertinent question, 'What has Johnny learned?' " (p. 179).

Alternatives to traditional grading available to school personnel who want distinctions to appear on report cards and transcripts for students who have different goals or who receive accommodations include pass/fail systems, student self-assessments, contracts with students, criterion or checklist grading, and portfolios. Indeed, some teachers choose to use these alternative assessment methods for all students. Another alternative is to use the IEP as the vehicle for grade determination. Students with disabilities have an advantage over other students in that they have an IEP, which, when used appropriately, clearly defines the objectives they are to reach, any accommodations required during instruction and assessment, and the criteria for determining grades.

The IEP is a powerful tool when working with school personnel reluctant to provide accommodations in instruction and assessment. Specifically, the IEP is a federal requirement, and federal law supersedes state and local laws, policies, and practices that might allow accommodations to be ignored. Perhaps, then, the questions we should really be asking here are, "Which students wouldn't benefit from accommodations and modifications in assessment based on learning style, multiple intelligences strengths, and differing interests?" and "If we accommodated for everyone and employed more of a portfolio approach through which students' actual performances and products were presented, what would be the purpose of grading and report cards?" These questions lead us away from discussion about whether or not students provided with accommodations should be given different grades and focus our thinking on "good teaching"—the identification and use of strategies to facilitate all children's learning.

9. Isn't inclusion in direct opposition to the national movement toward higher standards and outcomes for students? Teachers are expected to prepare students to score well on tests. Won't the presence of children with disabilities negatively impact the schools' scores and subsequently further erode public confidence in our school system?

The inclusion of children with disabilities is not in opposition to the movement to improve outcomes for students. On the contrary, both inclusive education and the call for higher standards at the federal, state, and local levels are attempts to foster conditions that will lead to better instruction and learning, equality of opportunity to learn, and excellence in performance for all children. Unfortunately, with few exceptions, the national educational reform initiatives of the past dozen years (including the higher standards movement) have failed to equalize learning opportunity or significantly alter student outcomes. Kenneth Howe (1994) suggests why when he concludes:

> It strains credulity . . . to suggest that implementing national standards and assessments could be anywhere near as effective a means of improving educational opportunity [or student outcomes] as addressing the conditions of schooling and society directly. It is rather like suggesting that the way to end world hunger is to first develop more rigorous standards of nutrition and then provide physicians with more precise means of measuring ratios of muscle-to-fat (p. 31).

We agree with Howe and suggest that the organizational, curricular, instructional, and assessment practices supportive of inclusive education described in this book hold greater promise for improved outcomes for children with *and* without disabilities than heightened national standards and associated assessments. These practices allow children with disabilities to thrive, to do as well or better than their counterparts in separate learning environments. Why wouldn't they have the same positive effect on other students?

As far as the concern that the presence of children with disabilities will negatively impact norm-referenced achievement scores—there is no evidence to validate this notion. In fact, studies suggest the contrary (Costello 1991; Cross and Villa 1992; Kaskinen-Chapman 1992; Sharpe, York, and Knight 1994; Staub and Peck 1994). "Effectiveness" can mean many things and, therefore, needs to be measured in a variety of ways and across a variety of curricular domains. However, one assessment approach—standardized, norm-referenced tests of achievement in traditional academic domains—remains the principal way schools communicate their effectiveness to the community. Interestingly, children with disabilities have not been part of the norming process for these tests and are routinely excluded (along with students enrolled in other "remedial" programs) in up to one-third of our schools' annual testing events. Because of such exclusionary evaluation practices, many communities are inadvertently making funding, policy, and programmatic decisions without full knowledge of the outcomes for all the children for whom they are responsible. The public is deceived when provided with "friendly" data indicating that schools are doing well. If public confidence in our schools is based on such practices, something is terribly wrong. A school has no business representing itself as effective unless it documents that it is effective for all children in its community.

Finally, the presence of children with disabilities in inclusive classrooms fits well with a goal of cooperation and competence, but may indeed thwart the purposes of those intent on social stratification and the survival of the fittest. Inclusive education calls many of the premises of our society and schools into question. This is precisely its value. Inclusive education forces us to ask ourselves, "What kinds of schools do we want?" and "What kind of a world do we want to live in?"

10. How can we guarantee the safety (physical and emotional) of the other students when a student with emotional or behavioral disabilities is placed in a general education classroom?

It is impossible to guarantee that every classroom, hallway, playground, lunchroom, and bus will always be completely safe. Violence is a problem in all aspects of North American society. There is violence in homes, on the streets, and in restaurants, malls, and workplaces. Concomitantly, an increasing number of children are perceived as troubled or troubling to their teachers, community, or family. More than 20 percent of U.S. children—the vast majority of whom are not special education eligible—carry a weapon to high school every day. Clearly, this is a societal problem and not solely education's responsibility.

Permanent solutions to student and societal violence will emerge only through community, interagency, and school collaboration. Yet, some solutions are emerging for addressing the needs of students with behavioral/emotional challenges and making schools more safe and welcoming learning environments.

First, the most effective and first "line of defense" against a student's rule-violating behavior is effective instruction with personalized accommodations and motivating learning experiences. Second, we need to develop a constellation of resources and services and bring them to students experiencing behavioral/emotional challenges. This constellation includes, but is not limited to, strategies for promoting and teaching responsibility and anger management and impulse control; social skills instruction; strategies for involving, empowering, and supporting students and family members; increased collaboration among and personal support for students from the adults at the school; and breaking with the traditional paradigm of schooling and what constitutes a student's day (see Villa, Udis, and Thousand 1994 for a detailed description of the constellation-of-services approach).

These and other supports and services for assisting students who are "troubled or troubling" can be brought to the school setting. It is unnecessary to send students away and immerse them in classroom or separate programs exclusively for children identified as emotionally or behaviorally challenging and counterproductive to send such students to a climate and culture of dysfunction and disturbance where they will have limited access to prosocial models of behavior and get a message that they do not belong with their peers (Kunc 1992). After all, children tend to live up to expectations, positive and negative. Isolation, incarceration, and exclusion set up a heartbreakingly vicious cycle. A person who feels a sense of alienation and exclusion is punished for giving evidence of lack of belonging through disruptive behavior by being further excluded and alienated, which then gives rise to accelerated rule-violating behavior. Is it any wonder that removing students with emotional/behavioral challenges from the regular classroom often results in increases in aggressive or violent behavior?

A basic responsibility of every school is to attempt to ensure students and adults freedom from physical harm. No student has the right to harm another person. Because there will inevitably be times when students place themselves and others in jeopardy, every school must have a well-articulated and well-understood crisis management system that promotes student responsibility and choice at each stage of a crisis. Choices within a crisis management system might include (a) allowing a student to "calm down" in a predetermined alternative setting in the school; (b) allowing students, with parental permission, to leave school grounds for a period of time; (c) in-school or out-of-school suspension for a short period of time until a team can convene and identify next steps; (d) removal of a student from school by a parent or by mental health, social service, or police personnel; and (e) use of passive physical restraint by trained personnel. We must remember that it is imperative that any student asked to leave school have a safe and supervised place to go.

Clearly, meeting the complex psychological and educational needs of students who are troubled or troubling is a difficult task. Matching intervention and support strategies to the life circumstances, stresses, and context from which an individual child operates requires thoughtful and careful consideration by teams of educators, parents, community members, and students who care about and are committed to the child's survival and success.

11. Inclusion would be nice, but it is unrealistic, if not impossible, given the situation that exists in our schools today. There is only one teacher per class. Student diversity is increasing. Public funding of education is decreasing. Class size is large; and, in some classes, 25–30 percent of children are identified as disabled. How can a teacher be expected to meet the needs of all children under such circumstances?

All the reasons for why inclusion is "impossible" referred to in this question have little if anything to do with children and everything to do with the way adults configure the delivery of their services. Given the cultural, racial, economic, and religious diversity of communities and students across the United States, the notion and practice of one educator working alone in a classroom is rapidly becoming outdated. In fact, it is probably the most impractical notion in education. A teacher working alone with traditional teaching methods (e.g., teacher-directed, predominantly independent or competitive student work structures, and the same performance standard for all children) is likely to be frustrated when attempting to accommodate increased student diversity. A strikingly different organizational structure—a teaching team—is necessary to meet the diverse needs of a heterogeneous student body.

Inclusive education redefines the role of the classroom teacher from the "lone ranger" to a "partner with supports." A teaching team is an organizational and instructional arrangement of two or more members of the school and greater community who share planning, instructional, and evaluation responsibilities for the same students on a regular basis over an extended period of time. According to Thousand and Villa (1990):

> Teams vary in size from two to six or seven people. They vary in composition as well, involving any possible combination of classroom teachers, specialized personnel (e.g., special educators, speech and language pathologists, guidance counselors, health professionals, employment specialists), instructional assistants, student teachers, community volunteers (e.g., parents, members of the local "foster grandparent" program), and students themselves (pp. 152–153).

This type of organizational structure capitalizes on the diverse experiences, knowledge bases, and instructional approaches of various team members (Bauwens, Hourcade, and Friend 1989) and allows for more immediate and accurate diagnosis of student needs and more active student learning.

Notably, an often-overlooked instructional and support resource in schools is the student body. In inclusive schools and classrooms, students are invited to be partners in various teaming arrangements (Thousand, Villa, and Nevin 1994; Villa and Thousand 1992). Students can function as *instructors* (e.g., cooperative group learning team members, peer tutors, co-instructors in teacher-student teaching teams, peer conflict mediators); *advocates* for themselves and peers (e.g., identifying learning outcomes; developing accommodations and modifications to curriculum, instruction, and assessment; serving as a support or a peer's "voice" in a transition planning meeting; helping develop social support networks); and *decision makers* (e.g., serving on school governance committees that develop school curriculums, inservice training programs, discipline policies, and organizational restructuring objectives).

In summary, for students with disabilities to be successful in general education classrooms, necessary supports and services must accompany them to the classroom. The supports and services are available if we choose to restructure and explore changes in roles and responsibilities of all members of the educational and greater community.

12. Won't children with disabilities be teased and ridiculed by the other children?

Probably some children will be teased, and they might do some teasing themselves, too. An unfortunate reality in many of our schools is that children face ridicule, teasing, and rejection. We would venture to guess that some of the readers of this book experienced teasing from peers during their school careers (e.g., on the playground, as a child; or in the faculty lounge, as a teacher). People are teased for many reasons, including differences in perceived abilities, physical characteristics, ethnic background, religion, language, culture, and socioeconomic status. Often, people make fun of what is new, unusual, or unfamiliar. Paradoxically, teasing sometimes can be a misguided attempt to express liking or attraction and build personal connections. The solution to the problem is not the removal of anyone who is different.

It is unlikely that adults will ever completely eliminate teasing and ridicule among children. There are, however, strategies to reduce it. Stainback and Stainback (1989, 1990) advocate a solution whereby educators instruct students about the valuing of individual differences and the importance of heterogeneous classroom experiences. They further suggest that teachers promote a caring ethic within their classrooms by establishing a "peer support committee" of rotating student membership. The mission of the committee is to determine ways for classmates to be supportive of one another.

Teachers can further reduce teasing by directly teaching children the reasons for and the results of name calling, teasing, and ridicule and by employing learning structures such as cooperative learning groups, which require and acknowledge positive treatment of classmates. Also, activities that stir concern for social justice have been effective in helping middle and high school students with little to no experience with persons with disabilities build support for and minimize teasing of students with disabilities. Engaging students in planning for the transition of a student with disabilities to become a welcomed member of their school community has had similar positive effects.

At the heart of the solution to teasing is teacher and administrator modeling. Students observe, reflect on, and imitate adult behavior toward people who are different and the problem-solving strategies they employ to deal with conflict and issues such as teasing and discrimination. Our experience has been that less ridicule occurs in inclusive schools. This might be due to a more explicit teaching of how to mediate conflict (Johnson, Johnson, Dudley, and Burnett 1992; Schrumpf 1994) and more problem solving when teasing and other forms of discrimination occur. Students who begin their educational careers with others with disabilities seem comfortable with and accepting of differences.

13. Are inclusion proponents advocating the elimination of professionals known as special educators? How will children's unique needs be

met in general education classrooms where they will not have access to therapists and other trained personnel?

Inclusion proponents are *not* calling for the elimination of special education or other specialists such as psychologists, physical and occupational therapists, and social workers. In fact, inclusionary environments *require* the participation of professionals who possess breadth and depth in many knowledge bases (e.g., human development and individual differences, particular reading or writing interventions, alternative communication strategies, mobility instruction, impulse control techniques). The goal is always to ensure that every student receives needed supports and resources. Therefore, what is being called for is a change in the way some specialized personnel deliver their expertise. Those who worked alone and pulled children away from general education are being asked to work together to figure out how to address students' needs in the context of general education. For specialists, this means being willing and able to take on the added responsibilities of becoming collaborators, models, coaches, and members of team teaching arrangements so as to pass on the essential elements of their specialty to teachers, parents, volunteers, students, and others. The end result is desegregation of adults and increased student access to the valuable services and expertise that specialists and classroom teachers can jointly provide.

14. What can I as one person do? I do not have the systems-level support needed to make inclusion work.

In an address to the young people of South Africa on their Day of Affirmation in 1966, Robert Kennedy stated (cited in Schlesinger 1987, p. 802):

> Some believe there is nothing one man or one woman can do against the enormous array of the world's ills, against ignorance, injustice, misery, or suffering. Yet many of the world's greatest movements, of thought and action, have flowed from the work of a single person. A young monk began the Protestant Reformation, a young general extended an empire from Macedonia to the borders of the earth, and a young woman reclaimed the territory of France. It was the 32-year-old Thomas Jefferson who proclaimed that all humans are created equal.

These people moved the world, and so can we all. Few will have the greatness to bend history itself, but each of us can work to change a small portion of events, and in the total of all of those acts will be written the history of this generation.

It is from the numberless diverse acts of courage and belief that human history is shaped. Each time a person stands up for an ideal, or acts to improve the lot of others, or strikes out against injustice, they send forth a tiny ripple of hope, and crossing each other from a million different centers of energy and daring, those ripples build a current that can sweep down the mightiest walls of oppression and resistance.

First, believe that you can make a difference, even though the system is not yet behind you. Next, act in any and every way you can think of to increase the number of people involved and the depth of their conviction to promote inclusion. How can this be done?

• Knowing that there is strength in numbers, build coalitions among disability rights, civil rights, parent, and other groups that will embrace an inclusive philosophy.

• Create support groups of families and others like yourself to strategize ways to get broader support.

• Locate or create a successful example of inclusion and showcase, share, and publicize it. Have people visit and talk with those involved in the effort.

• Get into positions of power. For example, run for the school board, become an officer of the teachers' union, or volunteer for committees that have influence to reform policy or practice in your school.

• Model through your own actions the inclusion of adults and children with diverse interests and abilities in your professional and personal life. To create a change, one must become the change.

• Educate others about the ethical, legal, moral, databased rationale for inclusive education. Share with them the information from Chapter 3 of this book, for instance.

• Persevere and be compassionate. Remember that changing people's minds and beliefs takes time and causes emotional turmoil.

• Take action now.

15. There are some children who need regular, intensive individualized instruction to acquire specific skills. How can the diverse needs of children with disabilities be met if we cannot take children out of general education classrooms for specific skill or functional life skill instruction?

In an inclusive school, it is expected that any student can and should receive focused and intensive instruction as needed. This instruction can occur in any location in the school that makes sense for the task, not a special location to which only students who are labeled or who get "special help" disappear for part of the day or week. Who delivers the focused instruction depends on any number of variables, such as professional expertise and interest or personal relationship with the child being instructed. Children, too, have proven to be exceptional at delivering focused instruction and should not be overlooked as instructional resources.

Part of the answer to meeting individualized learning needs lies in changing the nature of the general education classroom. When children are grouped heterogeneously and allowed to progress at their own pace without regard to age, grade, or level of ability or disability, individualization naturally occurs. Specialized instruction should be available to any child who might want or need it, but should never be based on a label attached to a child. Schools that embrace the belief that learning occurs in many forms in many different places have no trouble creatively designing ways to individualize for students.

16. How will children with disabilities come to understand that there are other people with disabilities similar to theirs if they are never given the opportunity to interact with people with disabilities? Aren't we sending contradictory messages? On the one hand, we are saying that it is all right to be different, while, on the other hand, we are telling students with disabilities that it isn't all right to associate with people who are similar to them because they need to be with people without disabilities.

Inclusion is about the right to freely associate, not about denying children with disabilities opportunities to know other people with similar disabilities or interests. The goal is to foster community, celebrate children's individual differences, and send the message that everyone has value. Allowing children to go to the same school as their siblings and neighbors does not suggest that they should or will not develop additional connections, relationships, and friendships outside of the classroom with people who have similar interests and characteristics.

Humans have a basic need to affiliate. In our society we have created all types of affiliation organizations (e.g., Italian-American associations, photography clubs) so people with common characteristics or interests can get together. Stainback, Stainback, and Sapon-Shevin (1994) and other multicultural education leaders stress the importance of developing positive self-identity for diverse groups of students within a school by supporting students' interests to affiliate with peers with similar characteristics. It is a responsibility of the school to create opportunities for children with disabilities to get together to share experiences, if they wish. As with other school clubs, these opportunities can occur during or outside of school hours. The key is to listen to the students, follow their lead, and help them to organize affiliations with the people they wish, for purposes of their choosing. Choice is essential. Adults should not impose a particular identity group (e.g., Down syndrome students) on children; only the students know their affiliation interests and solidarity needs. Further, a group's need for affiliation and solidarity should never be used as a rationale for segregation.

References

Bauwens, J., J.J. Hourcade, and M. Friend. (1989). "Cooperative Teaching: A Model for General and Special Education Integration." *Remedial and Special Education* 10, 2: 17–22.

Costello, C. (1991). "A Comparison of Student Cognitive and Social Achievement for Handicapped and Regular Education Students Who Are Educated in Integrated Versus a Substantially Separate Classroom." Unpublished doctoral diss., University of Massachusetts.

Cross, G., and R. Villa. (1992). "The Winooski School District." In *Restructuring for Caring and Effective Education: An Administrative Guide to Creating Heterogeneous Schools*, edited by R. Villa, J. Thousand, W. Stainback, and S. Stainback. Baltimore: Paul H. Brookes.

Doe, et al. v. Withers, 20 IDELR 422 (West Virginia Circuit Court, Taylor County, 1993).

Gardner, H. (1983). *Frames of Mind: The Theory of Multiple Intelligences*. New York: Basic Books.

Gardner, H. (1993). *Multiple Intelligences: The Theory in Practice*. New York: Basic Books.

Ginott, H. (1972). *Teacher and Child*. New York: Macmillan.

Howe, K. (1994). "Standards, Assessment, and Equality of Educational Opportunity." *Educational Researcher* 23, 8: 27–32.

Johnson, D., R. Johnson, B. Dudley, and R. Burnett. (1992). "Teaching Students to Be Peer Mediators. *Educational Leadership* 50, 1: 10–13.

Kaskinen-Chapman, A. (1992). "Saline Area Schools and Inclusive Community Concepts." In *Restructuring for Caring and Effective Education: An Administrative Guide to Creating Heterogeneous Schools*, edited by R. Villa, J. Thousand, W. Stainback, and S. Stainback. Baltimore: Paul H. Brookes.

Kunc, N. (1992). "The Need to Belong: Rediscovering Maslow's Hierarchy of Needs." In *Restructuring for Caring and Effective Education: An Administrative Guide to Creating Heterogeneous Schools*, edited by R. Villa, J. Thousand, W. Stainback, and S. Stainback. Baltimore: Paul H. Brookes.

Lilly, M.S. (1971). "A Training Based Model for Special Education." *Exceptional Children* 37: 745–749.

Nevin, A., R. Villa, and J. Thousand. (1992). "An Invitation to Invent the Extraordinary: A Response to Morsink." *Remedial and Special Education* 13, 6: 44–46.

Noddings, N. (1992). *The Challenge to Care in Schools*. New York: Teachers College Press.

"No More School, No More Books . . . and We Miss It." (June 5, 1994). *Arizona Republic*, Kids Page. (Phoenix, Ariz.).

Reynolds, M.C. (1962). "A Framework for Considering Some Issues in Special Education." *Exceptional Children* 28: 267–270.

Reynolds, M.C. (1977). "The Instructional Cascade." In *The Least Restrictive Alternative: Vol. 4, Leadership Series in Special Education*, edited by A. Rehnam and T. Riggen. Minneapolis: University of Minnesota, Audio-Visual Library Series.

Sapon-Shevin, M. (1994). *Playing Favorites: Gifted Education and the Disruption of Community*. Albany: State University of New York Press.

Schlesinger, A.M. Jr. (1978). *Robert Kennedy and His Times*. New York: Ballantine Books.

Schrumpf, F. (1994). "The Role of Students in Resolving Conflicts." In *Creativity and Collaborative Learning: A Practical Guide to Empowering Students and Teachers*, edited by J.S. Thousand, R.A. Villa, and A.I. Nevin. Baltimore: Paul H. Brookes.

Sharpe, N., J. York, and J. Knight. (1994). "Effects of Inclusion on the Academic Performance of Classmates Without Disabilities: A Preliminary Study." *Remedial and Special Education* 15, 5: 281–287.

Shriner, J., J. Ysseldyke, M. Thurlow, and D. Honetschlager. (1994). "'All Means All'—Including Students with Disabilities." *Educational Leadership* 51, 6: 38–42.

Slavin, R. (1987). "Ability Grouping and Achievement in Elementary School: A Best Evidence Synthesis." *Review of Educational Research* 57: 293–336.

Stainback, W., and S. Stainback. (1989). "Common Concerns Regarding Merger." In *Educating All Students in the Mainstream of Regular Education*, edited by S. Stainback, W. Stainback, and M. Forest. Baltimore: Paul H. Brookes.

Stainback, W., and S. Stainback. (1990). "Facilitating Peer Supports and Friendships." In *Support Networks for Inclusive Schooling: Interdependent Integrated Education*, edited by W. Stainback and S. Stainback. Baltimore: Paul H. Brookes.

Stainback, S., W. Stainback, and M. Sapon-Shevin. (1994). "A Commentary on Inclusion and the Development of a Positive Self-Identity by People with Disabilities." *Exceptional Children* 60, 6: 486–490.

Staub, D., and C. Peck. (1994). "What Are the Outcomes for Nondisabled Students?" *Educational Leadership* 52, 4: 36–40.

Thousand, J. (1990). "Organizational Perspectives on Teacher Education Renewal: A Conversation with Tom Skrtic." *Teacher Education and Special Education* 13, 1: 30–35.

Thousand, J., and R. Villa. (1990). "Sharing Expertise and Responsibilities Through Teaching Teams." In *Support Networks for Inclusive Schooling: Integrated Interdependent Education*, edited by W. Stainback and S. Stainback. Baltimore: Paul H. Brookes.

Thousand, J., R. Villa, H. Meyers, and A. Nevin. (April 1994). "The Heterogeneous Education Teacher Survey: A Retrospective Analysis of Heterogeneous (Full Inclusion) Education." Paper presented at the annual American Education Research Association convention, New Orleans.

Thousand, J., R. Villa, and A. Nevin. (1994). *Creativity and Collaborative Learning: A Practical Guide to Empowering Students and Teachers*. Baltimore: Paul H. Brookes.

Van der Klift, E., and N. Kunc. (1994). "Friendship and the Politics of Help." In *Creativity and Collaborative Learning: A Practical Guide to Empowering Students and Teachers*, edited by J.S. Thousand, R.A. Villa, and A.I. Nevin. Baltimore: Paul H. Brookes.

Vermont State Department of Education. (1993). *Vermont's Common Core of Learning*. Montpelier: Author

Villa, R., and J. Thousand. (1992). "Student Collaboration: An Essential for Curriculum Delivery in the 21st Century." In *Curriculum Considerations for Inclusive Classrooms: Facilitating Learning for All Students*, edited by S. Stainback and W. Stainback. Baltimore: Paul H. Brookes.

Villa, R., J. Udis, and J. Thousand. (1994). "Responses for Children Experiencing Behavioral and Emotional Challenges." In *Creativity and Collaborative Learning: A Practical Guide to Empowering Students and Teachers*, edited by J. Thousand, R. Villa, and A.I. Nevin. Baltimore: Paul H. Brookes.

Voice of Inclusion: In Spite of My Disability

Norman Kunc and Emma Van der Klift

Norm: Emma and I were invited to speak at a conference on inclusive education. After one of our workshops, a young woman approached Emma. On the verge of tears, she explained that she had a 10-year-old son with cerebral palsy. "Until today," she said, "I never thought about the possibility of marriage, or even a loving relationship for him with anybody but his family. Seeing you with Norm has changed all that. Thank you." Emma smiled and reached out to touch her shoulder.

Then, the kicker. "I think it's amazing that you love Norm *in spite of his disability.*"

Amazing? In spite of my disability? I overheard and felt insulted, overwhelmed by the implications of her comment. One more time, relegated to the subhuman. Not a real man.

I was filled with an overwhelming urge to "educate" this woman— through retaliation. I tried to invoke my undergraduate training in rhetoric and debate as I approached her. A suitably caustic response was forming in my mind.

Luckily, Emma saw my approach in time. She could tell by my increased spasticity that I had overheard and was in revenge mode. She stepped deftly in front of me, blocked my path, and said to the woman, "I don't think you understand. I don't love Norm in spite of his disability. I love Norm. Period. His disability is a part of him. I can't imagine who Norm would be without his disability."

The woman walked away obviously confused. Emma turned to me. "Feel like a double scotch?" she asked. We left in search of the bar.

Emma: It's not really that simple. The truth is, I never get used to it. A quick karate chop to the esophagus. A sharp smack on the psyche.

Norm: Needless to say, Emma saved me from weeks of self-recrimination and guilt, to say nothing of how I might have wounded that woman. To be fair to myself, I'm usually more understanding than I would have been that day. I know there is no excuse for retaliation, especially as vicious as mine was going to be. Nevertheless, the words "in spite of" reveal the difficulty this woman had in seeing me as a person, let alone a man. In her mind, I seemed to be a collection of abnormal speech patterns and involuntary movements. Trapped behind an opaque wall of cerebral palsy, it was impossible to correct the vision, let alone explore what we might have in common.

Situations like these happen all the time. People make unwarranted assumptions and inferences about who I am as a person or what my life is like, solely on the basis of my disability. Many people, for example, assume that all people with cerebral palsy have a limited intellect. Therefore, when they meet me, they assume I have a mental disability. Some people think cerebral palsy is a disease, so they don't want to touch me, in case they catch it. Still others see me as a charity case, someone to feel sorry for.

Emma: Assumptions and inferences—polite words for prejudice.

Norm: When people first meet me, they tend to see me as nine-tenths disability and one-tenth person. What they see as paramount are the things that mark me as "different"—the way I walk, speak, and move. My disability expands in their eyes, throwing a shadow over me and my life in the same way that a shadow on a sundial widens in the afternoon light. They perceive my disability as having more of an influence over me than it *actually* does.

Let me counteract that view for a moment, and describe myself to you as I see myself. I'm a white male who grew up in Toronto, Canada. My father is Polish, my mother English. I have an older brother and sister, and nieces and nephews. Our family is Anglican, but I grew up in a predominantly Jewish neighborhood. I earned an undergraduate degree in Humanities and a Master of Science degree in Family Therapy. I like sailing, and I used to compete in local and regional races. I'm married to Emma and live in Port Alberni, British Columbia. I am a stepdad to Jodi, Erinn, and Evan. We live in an old house we've renovated and love. Emma and I have our own business as consultants. We share a passionate interest in social justice and conflict management. I enjoy computers, classical music, and Greek food. I play the drums, although not well. I have an uncanny ability to remember phone numbers and jokes. I also have cerebral palsy.

Emma: I have an affectionate recollection of Norm and Evan. In this scene, Evan is about five years old. The two of them are repairing the brass fireplace surround, an odd, rickety thing that I've carried around from house to house with me for years simply because I like its funny, art-deco shape. Unfortunately, in addition to its charm, it mysteriously loses its stabilizing screws on a regular basis.

Norm is replacing the screws laboriously, but since fine-motor control is not his strong suit, it's a difficult task. "Would you help me, Evan?" he asks. After explaining what has to be done, he watches as Evan carefully puts the screws in.

"I know why you need me." Evan says proudly. "It's 'cause you're wiggly, right, Norm?"

"That's right, Evan. I'm wiggly." An unusual, though apt, description of cerebral palsy.

"I'm not wiggly," Evan goes on, "but I'm not too strong yet, either. You're wiggly but you're strong. You can pick up big heavy things. . . ." He walks away, musing about this apparent paradox.

Norm: Cerebral palsy is a small part of who I am as a person and what my life is about. I've become so accustomed to making daily accommodations for my disability that I often forget that I have one. When it does come into my awareness, I simply see it as part of my life. I honestly don't think about my disability that much. It's boring. There are other things to think about.

The "in spite of" comment not only implied an exaggerated view of my disability, it also presumed a deficiency within me. The inferences people make about my disability reveal more about their stereotypical views about the *idea of disability* than about the limitations of a disability itself. For the woman who made that comment, I was simply a defective adult, a grown-up version of her defective child. I was abnormal, and although deserving of kindness and sympathy, fundamentally "different." Slightly beneath her words, the unspoken insult was clear. Why would anyone marry a man with a disability? He's ugly, he's broken, not quite fully human. What could he possibly offer anyone? He'd be a burden. If I were married to him, would others think that I couldn't do any better?

Emma: When I tell people this story or one of hundreds like it that center around the deliberate or accidental insensitivity of nondisabled people, I am both amused and distressed at the reactions I get.

"You have to understand," they say. I always know what's coming whenever I hear that phrase. I usually want to sigh when I hear it. Sometimes *understanding* is very tiring, especially when you "have to."

"She didn't mean it," they often add. "She just doesn't know any better. In fact, she does it to everyone."

Admittedly, this can be true. I actually do know that most people who do or say silly things don't mean to be offensive. I know that often they are just trying to be helpful, but operate out of a set of assumptions based in myth, misinformation, or a lack of information. And I also know that unfortunately, some people really do treat almost everyone (with the possible exception of those they perceive as more powerful) with condescension and a lack of respect. I sometimes wonder if the people who listen to my stories don't think I know these things. Maybe that's why they feel that it's their personal responsibility to edit my experience and provide me with a more "balanced" interpretation of events.

Have I lost my perspective? Have I become unkind? I hope not. I do my share of embarrassingly ignorant things. Most of the stories I tell are not without humor and perspective. I try not to blame people, or fall prey to the "evil oppressor/victim" stereotypes. So why the knee-jerk reaction? Why do I get 10-minute sermons on offering up the other cheek?

It occurs to me that there's more going on here than meets the eye. There's a message underneath the message. When people ask me to "understand" the ignorance and prejudice of others and swallow my pain, they are asking me to be quiet. They're saying, "It's not really like that. You're imagining things. You're overreacting. You're paranoid."

I guess I can't accept that it's okay for people to continue not to know any better. Silence and compulsive "understanding" never did much to challenge or change the status quo.

Norm: I'm sometimes asked, "You've accomplished so much in your life with a disability. Have you ever wondered where you'd be if you hadn't had cerebral palsy?"

For me, the answer is obvious. I'd be a drummer in a blues band. I work on social justice issues because I can't do triplets on a ride cymbal.

An overstatement, obviously—yet it's truthful enough to engender a moment of existential reflection. Would I have followed a life of speaking and writing about human rights issues if the world of musical composition and performance was open to me? I honestly don't know.

Given what I know now, however, if I were offered a choice, I would choose to live *with* cerebral palsy. This statement invariably evokes bewilderment and skepticism among nondisabled people. They are firmly convinced that I would be "better off"—and hence, prefer—to live a nondisabled life. What they fail to understand is that cerebral palsy is an integral part of who I am. My identity is the product of my history. My history is that of a person with cerebral palsy. If I didn't have cerebral palsy, I wouldn't be who I am; I'd be someone else. Frankly, I like who I am, I like my history, I like my life. I'm not sure I'd sacrifice who I am for the sake of normal movement and speech.

Many people assume that living with cerebral palsy means that I am endlessly confronted by my body's limitations. Actually, this is not my experience. Having cerebral palsy means living a life in which innovation, improvisation, creativity, and lateral thinking are essential. In practical terms, it means knowing which cup fits snugly into the sink drain and doesn't tip over when I pour coffee. It means finding the same challenge and enjoyment in keeping my balance on an icy sidewalk that my friends find when they master Tai Chi. It means being ever-conscious of the number of drinking straws in my possession in the same way that a smoker is always aware of the remaining number of cigarettes. It means paying attention to breathing and articulation, like a jazz singer crafting a phrase. It means bracing my wrist on the table before I grasp a glass of wine in the same way that Emma braces her left hand when she threads a needle. As far as I know, Emma does not long to be a brain surgeon every time the eye of the needle eludes her thread.

Emma: I don't have a disability. Norm does. We have to negotiate both a personal and a professional relationship. This presents some interesting dilemmas: Who does what? What's a fair division of labor? Conventional solutions to the "fairness" dilemma just don't work for us. We've had to reinvent the rules. It's like street theater—we're continuously improvising. We change the rules or make up new ones as we go.

Cooking is difficult for Norm. It isn't that he can't, but it requires an inordinate amount of effort, planning, balance, and innovation. At the right time, cooking can be a challenge, an interesting problem to solve. Mostly, it's arduous and time consuming. On the other hand, I love to cook. For me, it's cathartic, creative, and different enough from what I do for a living to provide me with a much-needed reprieve. So I cook. I also clean. Norm lifts heavy things. He takes the garbage out. He also takes care of office and travel trivia and returns more calls than I do.

Sometimes our roles appear deceptively traditional and gender specific; sometimes they don't. For example, I read a lot. Norm reads less. I'm primarily a divergent thinker, he's more convergent. I become overwhelmed by the sheer volume of what I have read; Norm has an incredible ability to create coherence out of chaos. Rather than undertaking lifelong remediation with each other, we use our differences in complementary ways. I still can't believe that a valuable part of our work together involves the luxury of reading! I read and highlight; Norm synthesizes; we both write. Our work is stronger. We're happier. Our strengths are utilized, and our weaknesses seem more irrelevant. Interestingly, our continued collaboration has helped me to become more organized—and Norm is reading more.

In the quest to figure out what equality means, many of us confuse it with symmetry. The commonly accepted definition of "fair" seems to be "a tidy thwack down the middle of everything." It's as if we believe that equality can be mandated, maintained, and meted out by an exacting and humorless accountant. Norm and I have decided to take a longer view of equity. We know it isn't about treating people the same or ending up with a carefully balanced sheet at the end of each day. It's about quality of life, negotiation, interdependence, and long-term relationships. We're learning that giving means contributing *what* you can *where* you can, without obsessing about what you don't have or can't do. We know that what we get back is often unexpected, generous, and complementary. We create a different kind of climate—life is less structured and more fun. Imagination, flexibility, and humor are a bigger part of our lives—things few people feel they have enough of.

Would I have learned these things if Norm weren't disabled? I'd like to think so, but I'm not sure. Working on the pragmatic level, solving problems that relate to physical differences, has helped us learn skills we can translate and use on a more conceptual level. It's not just about how to manage daily life with a disability. It's bigger than that. It's a whole new way of thinking about how we orchestrate our relationships and our lives.

"One-answer" thinking seldom works for us, so we've learned to look for multiple alternatives to the "usual" way of getting things done. As a result, when solutions can't be found inside conventional modalities, we're remembering to look for different ones. Even if the old answers do fit, we're more inclined to wonder if those are the solutions we *really* need, or just the ones we're used to. We are looking for wider spaces and new models large enough to hold us; synergistic and complementary enough to sustain us. We are always reshaping and reinterpreting our lives. I wouldn't have it any other way.

8

Resources for Advancing Inclusive Education

Barbara E. Buswell and C. Beth Schaffner

Lack of information is a common barrier to successful inclusive education. Most general educators, and even many special educators, are unfamiliar with effective strategies for educating students with disabilities outside of separate special classrooms. Some teachers may be hesitant to have students with disabilities in their classrooms because they have not seen examples of successful inclusive education in practice or talked to anyone who's taught in an inclusive classroom. In addition, many people are unaware that the proposed reforms for general education are the same kinds of instructional approaches that support successful inclusion of students with disabilities.

Good resources can remedy this lack of knowledge and help teachers and parents understand how inclusive education works. Many informative publications on inclusion are available, as are a number of videos demonstrating ways to support students with disabilities in general education classrooms. In fact, there are so many resources that educators and parents frequently find it difficult to assess which materials might be most useful in their particular setting.

When selecting materials, it is important to consider the audience's level of familiarity with the concept of inclusive education. For people just beginning to think about inclusion, resource materials should be brief, clear, and free of special education jargon. Materials should frame the big issues involved and also directly address strategies that support students, so that people can see how schools can successfully accommodate diverse students in neighborhood schools and general education classrooms. In addition, resource materials should address issues directly, so that people new to these issues will understand how the information applies to the inclusion of students with disabilities.

Resources can be used in many ways. Frequently, people who are introducing inclusion to their school, district, or community provide basic information by distributing brief articles to teachers, support people, school board members, key administrators, and families. Some parents have made appointments with their neighborhood school principal to watch brief videos about inclusion and then discuss with the principal strategies from the video that might work particularly well to support *their* child. Videos and slides in which students with disabilities are participating with typical peers in general education activities, with supports provided, are particularly useful for such meetings.

Many groups are emerging as reliable resources for information on inclusive educational strategies. Particular groups to consider contacting include:

• The Association for Persons with Severe Handicaps (TASH), 29 Susquehanna Ave., Suite 210, Baltimore, MD 21204. Phone: (410) 828-8274. Fax: (410) 828-6706.

• Association for Supervision and Curriculum Development (ASCD), 1250 N. Pitt St., Alexandria, VA 22314. Phone: (703) 549-9110. Fax: (703) 549-3891 or 836-7921.

• National Association of State Boards of Education (NASBE), 1012 Cameron St., Alexandria, VA 22314. Phone: (800) 220-5183. Fax: (703) 836-2313.

• National Education Association (NEA), 1201 16th St., N.W., Washington, DC 20036. Phone: (202) 833-4000. Fax: (no central fax).

In some states, one can approach people who have particular experience and expertise in supporting inclusive education in universities, private consultants, federally funded systems change projects, parent training and information centers, developmental disabilities planning councils, and state departments of education. Many states host yearly conferences and institutes that focus on strategies for successfully including students with disabilities.

The remainder of this chapter identifies topical areas related to inclusion and resources to assist the reader in creating inclusive classrooms and school communities. Due to limited space, the materials listed are, for the most part, intended to supplement those appearing in the chapter reference lists in this book. Readers who desire a more comprehensive resource list should write to the PEAK Parent Center, 6055 Lehman Dr., Colorado Springs, CO 80918, or call (719) 531-9400.

General Resources on Inclusion

Books

See Chapter 4 for additional resources.

Biklen, D., D. L. Ferguson, and A. Ford. (1989). *Schooling and Disability.* Chicago: National Society for the Study of Education. 287 pp.

Dillon, A., C. Tashie, M. Schuh, C. Jorgensen, S. Shapiro-Barnard, B. Dixon, and J. Nisbet, eds. (1993). *Treasures—A Celebration of Inclusion.* Concord, N.H.: University of New Hampshire, Institute on Disability, The Concord Center, Box 14, 10 Ferry St., Concord, NH 03301.

Lipsky, D.K., and A. Gartner, eds. (1989). *Beyond Separate Education: Quality Education for All.* Baltimore: Paul H. Brookes. 302 pp.

O'Brien, J., M. Forest, J. Snow, and D. Hasbury. (1989). *Action for Inclusion: How to Improve Schools by Welcoming Children with Special Needs into Regular Classrooms.* Toronto: Frontier College Press. 54 pp.

Tashie, C., S. Shapiro-Barnard, M. Schuh, C. Jorgensen, A. Dillon, B. Dixon, and J. Nisbet. (1993). *From Special to Regular, From Ordinary to Extraordinary.* Concord, N.H.: University of New Hampshire, Institute on Disability, The Concord Center, Box 14, 10 Ferry St., Concord, NH 03301.

Articles and Reports

Biklen, D. (1988). "The Myth of Clinical Judgment." *Journal of Social Issues* **44**, 1: 127-140.

Blackman, H.P. (1989). "Special Education Placement: Is It What You Know or Where You Live?" *Exceptional Children* 55, 5: 459-462.

Lipsky, D., and A. Gartner. (1988). "Capable of Achievement and Worthy of Respect: Education for Handicapped Students as if They Were Full-fledged Human Beings." *Exceptional Children* 54, 1: 69-74.

National Association of State Boards of Education. (1992). *Winners All: A Call for Inclusive Schools.* Alexandria, Va.: NASB.

National Center on Educational Restructuring and Inclusion. (Spring 1994). *National Survey on Inclusive Education.* Number 1. New York: The Graduate School and University Center.

Rogers, J. (May 1993). *The Inclusion Revolution.* Research Bulletin, Number 11, pp. 1-6. Bloomington, Ind.: Phi Delta Kappa Center for Evaluation, Development, and Research.

Stainback, S., and W. Stainback. (1988). "Educating Students with Severe Disabilities." *Teaching Exceptional Children* 21, 1: 16-19.

Taylor, S. (1988). "Caught in the Continuum: A Critical Analysis of the Principle of the Least Restrictive Environment." *Journal of the Association for Persons with Severe Handicaps* 13, 1: 41-53.

Wang, M., M. Reynolds, and H. Walberg. (November 1988). "Integrating the Children of the Second System." *Phi Delta Kappan* 70, 3: 248-251.

Will, M. (1986). *Educating Students with Learning Problems—A Shared Responsibility.* Washington, D.C.: U.S. Department of Education, Office of Special Education and Rehabilitative Services. 23 pp.

Laws and Court Decisions

Gilhool, T. (1989). "The Right to an Effective Education: From Brown to PL 94-142 and Beyond." In *Beyond Separate Education: Quality Education for All,* edited by D. Lipsky and A. Gartner. Baltimore: Paul H. Brookes.

Laski, F., J. Gran, and P. Boyd. (1993). *Oberti v. Clementon.* Philadelphia: Public Interest Law Center of Philadelphia.

Laski, F. (June 1994). "On the 40th Anniversary of Brown v. Board of Education: Footnotes for the Historically Impaired." *TASH Newsletter* 20, 6.

Lipton, D. (1994). *The Full Inclusion Court Cases.* New York: National Center on Educational Restructuring and Inclusion, Graduate School and University, City University of New York.

Hasazi, S.B., A.P. Johnston, A.M. Liggett, and R.A. Schattman. (1994). "A Qualitative Policy Study of the Least Restrictive Environment Provision of the Individuals with Disabilities Education Act." *Exceptional Children* 60, 6: 491-507.

United States Court of Appeals for the Ninth Circuit. (1994). *Sacramento Unified School District v. Holland.* San Francisco: Barclays Law Publishers.

Research Articles

See Chapter 3 for additional resources.

Baker, E., M. Wang, and H. Walberg. (December 1994). "The Effects of Inclusion on Learning." *Educational Leadership* 52, 4: 33-35.

Danielson, L.C., and G.T. Bellamy. (1989). "State Variation in Placement of Children with Handicaps in Segregated Environments." *Exceptional Children* 55, 5: 448-455.

Giangreco. M.F., R. Dennis, C. Cloninger, S. Edelman, and R. Schattman. (1993). "I've Counted Jon: Transformational Experiences of Teachers Educating Students with Disabilities." *Exceptional Children* 59, 4: 359-372.

Halvorsen, A., and W. Sailor. (1990). "Integration of Students with Severe and Profound Disabilities: A Review of Research." In *Issues and Research in Special Education*, Vol. 1, edited by R. Gaylord-Ross. New York: Teachers College Press.

Meadows, N., R. Neel, C. Scott, and G. Parker. (1994). "Academic Performance, Social Competence, and Mainstream Accommodations: A Look at Mainstreamed and Nonmainstreamed Students with Serious Behavioral Disorders." *Behavioral Disorders* 19, 3: 170-180.

Salisbury, C., M. Palombaro, and T. Hollowood. (1993). "On the Nature and Change of an Inclusionary Elementary School." *Journal of the Association for Persons with Severe Handicaps* 18, 2: 75-84.

Schnorr, R.F. (1990). "Peter? He Comes and Goes: First Graders' Perspective on a Part-Time Mainstream Student." *Journal of the Association for Persons with Severe Handicaps* 15, 4: 231-340.

Straub, D., and C. Peck. (December 1994). "What Are the Outcomes for Nondisabled Students?" *Educational Leadership* 52, 4: 36-40.

Wagner, M. (1989). "Youth with Disabilities During Transition: An Overview and Description of Findings from the National Longitudinal Transition Study." In *Transition Institute at Illinois: Project Director's Fourth Annual Meeting*, edited by J. Chadsey-Rusch. Champaign, Ill.: University of Illinois.

School Reform and Inclusive Education

Books

See Chapter 4 for additional resources.

Armstrong, T. (1994). *Multiple Intelligences in the Classroom*. Alexandria, Va.: ASCD.

Barth, R.S. (1990). *Improving Schools from Within*. San Francisco, Calif.: Jossey-Bass.

Brown, R. (1991). *Schools of Thought: How the Politics of Literacy Shape Thinking in the Classroom*. San Francisco: Jossey-Bass.

Connell, R. (1993). *Schools and Social Justice*. Philadelphia: Temple University Press.

Eisner, E.W. (1994). *Cognition and Curriculum Reconsidered*. New York: Teachers College Press.

Gardner, H. (1992). *The Unschooled Mind: How Children Think and How Schools Should Teach.* New York: Basic Books.

Glasser, W. (1990). *The Quality School: Managing Students Without Coercion.* New York: Harper and Row.

Goodlad, J., and T. Lovitt. (1993). *Integrating General and Special Education.* New York: Macmillan.

Kohn, A. (1993). *Punished by Rewards.* New York: Houghton Mifflin.

Kozol, J. (1991). *Savage Inequalities: Children in America's Schools.* New York: HarperCollins.

National Coalition of Advocates for Students. (1991). *The Good Common School: Making the Vision Work for All Children.* Boston: National Coalition of Advocates for Students.

National Education Association. (1994). *Toward Inclusive Classrooms.* West Haven, Conn.: NEA Professional Libraries.

Oakes, J. (1985). *Keeping Track: How Schools Structure Inequality.* New Haven, Conn.: Yale University Press.

Schlechty, P. (1990). *Schools for the 21st Century: Leadership Imperatives for Educational Reform.* San Francisco: Jossey-Bass.

Senge, P. (1990). *The Fifth Discipline: The Art and Practice of the Learning Organization.* New York: Doubleday/Currency.

Sergiovanni, T. (1992). *Moral Leadership: Getting to the Heart of the Matter.* San Francisco: Jossey-Bass.

Wheelock, A. (1992). *Crossing the Tracks: How "Untracking" Can Save America's Schools.* New York: The New Press.

Articles and Reports

Brandt, R. (October 1993). "On Restructuring Roles and Relationships: A Conversation with Phil Schlechty." *Educational Leadership* 51, 2: 8-11.

Educational Leadership. (December 1994/January 1995). Theme issue on "The Inclusive School." 52, 4: entire issue. (Available from ASCD.)

Eisner, E.W. (February 1991). "What Really Counts in Schools." *Educational Leadership* 48, 5: 10-17.

Strategies for Administrators

Books

See Chapter 5 for additional resources.

Sage, D., and L. Burrello. (1994). *Leadership in Educational Reform.* Baltimore: Paul H. Brookes.

Villa, R.A., J.S. Thousand, W. Stainback, and S. Stainback. (1992). *Restructuring for Caring and Effective Education: An Administrative Guide to Creating Heterogeneous Schools.* Baltimore: Paul H. Brookes.

Articles and Reports

Schattman, R., and J. Benay. (1992). "Inclusive Practices Transform Special Education in the 1990s." *The School Administrator* 49, 2: 8-13.

Skrtic, T. (1991). "Students with Special Educational Needs: Artifacts of the Traditional Curriculum." In *Effective Schools for All,* edited by M. Ainscow. London: David Fulton.

Villa, R., and J. Thousand. (1990). "Administrative Supports to Promote Inclusive Schooling." In *Support Networks for Inclusive Schooling: Interdependent Integrated Education,* edited by W. Stainback and S. Stainback. Baltimore: Paul H. Brookes.

Villa, R.A., and J.S. Thousand. (October 1992). "How One District Integrated Special and General Education." *Educational Leadership* 50, 2: 39-41.

Curriculum Adaptations and Teaching Strategies

Books

See Chapters 5 and 6 for additional resources.

Fagen, S.A., D.L. Graves, and D. Tessier-Switlick. (1984). *Promoting Successful Mainstreaming.* Rockville, Md: Montgomery County Public Schools.

Falvey, M. (in press). *Inclusive and Heterogeneous Schooling: Assessment, Curriculum, and Instruction.* Baltimore: Paul H. Brookes.

Putnam, J. ed. (1993). *Cooperative Learning and Strategies for Inclusion.* Baltimore: Paul H. Brookes.

Schaffner, C.B., and B.E. Buswell. (1991). *Opening Doors: Strategies for Including All Students in Regular Education.* Colorado Springs: PEAK Parent Center, Inc.

Thousand, J., R. Villa, and A. Nevin, eds. (1994). *Creativity and Collaborative Learning: A Practical Guide to Empowering Students and Teachers.* Baltimore: Paul H. Brookes.

Wang, M. (1991). *Adaptive Education Strategies: Building on Diversity.* Baltimore Paul H. Brookes.

Articles and Reports

Jorgensen, C. (Spring 1994). "Creating Questions That All Students Can Answer: A Key to Developing Inclusive Curriculum." *Equity and Excellence* 2, 1: 22-27. (Available from Institute on Disability, Heidelberg-Harris Building, University of New Hampshire, Durham, NH 03824.)

Silva, P. (Spring 1993). "Starting the Fire in the Heterogeneous Classroom." *Equity and Excellence* 1, 1: 4-5. (Available from Institute on Disability, Heidelberg-Harris Building, University of New Hampshire, Durham, NH 03824.)

Villa, R., and J. Thousand. (in press). "Student Collaboration: An Essential for Curriculum Delivery in the 21st Century." In *Handbook of Practical Strategies for Inclusive Schooling*, edited by S. Stainback and W. Stainback. Baltimore: Paul H. Brookes.

Collaborative Teaming and Planning Processes

Books

Giangreco, M.F., C.J. Cloninger, and G.S. Iverson. (1993). *Choosing Options and Accommodations for Children (COACH): A Guide to Planning Inclusive Education*. Baltimore: Paul H. Brookes.

Idol, L., A. Nevin, and P. Paolucci-Whitcomb. (1994). *Collaborative Consultation*, 2nd. ed. Austin, Texas: Pro-Ed.

Rainforth, B., J. York, and C. Macdonald. (1992). *Collaborative Teams for Students with Severe Disabilities: Integrating Therapy and Educational Services*. Baltimore: Paul H. Brookes.

Tashie, C., S. Shapiro-Barnard, A. Dillon, M. Schuh, C. Jorgensen, and J. Nisbet. (1993). *Changes in Attitudes, Changes in Latitudes: The Role of the Inclusion Facilitator*. Concord, N.H.: University of New Hampshire, Institute on Disability, The Concord Center Box 14, 10 Ferry St., Concord NH 03301.

Articles and Reports

Forest, M., and J. Pearpoint. (October 1992). "Putting All Kids on the Map. *Educational Leadership* 50, 2: 26-31.

Giangreco, M.F., C.J. Cloninger, R. Dennis, and S. Edelman. (1994). "Problem-solving Methods to Facilitate Inclusive Education." In *Creativity and Collaborative Learning: A Practical Guide to Empowering Students and Teachers*, edited by J. Thousand, R. Villa, and A. Nevin. Baltimore: Paul H. Brookes.

Harris, K.C. (1990). "Meeting Diverse Needs Through Collaborative Consultation." In *Support Networks for Inclusive Schooling: Interdependent Integrated Education*, edited by W. Stainback and S. Stainback. Baltimore: Paul H. Brookes.

Thousand, J., and R. Villa. (1992). "Collaborative Teams: A Powerful Tool in School Restructuring." In *Restructuring for Caring and Effective Education: An Administrative Guide to Creating Heterogeneous Schools*, edited by R. Villa, J. Thousand, W. Stainback, and S. Stainback. Baltimore: Paul H. Brookes.

Thousand, J., R. Villa, P. Paolucci-Whitcomb, and A. Nevin. (in press). "A Rationale and Vision for Collaborative Consultation." In *Controversial Issues Confronting Special Education: Divergent Perspectives*, 2nd ed. edited by W. Stainback and S. Stainback. Boston: Allyn and Bacon.

Behavior Support Strategies

Books

Brendtro, L., M. Brokenleg, and S. Van Bockern. (1990). *Reclaiming Youth At Risk: Our Hope for the Future.* Bloomington, Ind.: National Educational Service.
Curwin, R., and A. Mendler, A. (1988). *Discipline with Dignity.* Alexandria, Va.: ASCD.
Goldstein, A. (1988). *The Prepare Curriculum.* Champaign, Ill.: Research Press.
Hamilton, R., J. Welkowitz, M. deOlivia, S. Prue, and T. Fox. (1995). *Prevention, Teaching, and Responding: A Planning Process for Supporting Students with Emotional and Behavioral Difficulties in Regular Education.* Burlington, Vt.: The University Affiliated Program of Vermont.
Knitzer, J., Z. Steinberg, and B. Fleisch. (1990). *At the Schoolhouse Door: An Examination of Programs and Policies for Children with Behavioral and Emotional Problems.* New York: Bank Street College of Education.
McGee, J.J., F.J. Menolascino, D.C. Hobbs, and P.E. Menousek. (1987). *Gentle Teaching.* New York: Human Sciences Press.
Mendler, A. (1992). *What Do I Do When? How to Achieve Discipline with Dignity in the Classroom.* Bloomington, Ind.: National Educational Service.
Meyer, L.J., and I.M. Evans. (1989). *Nonaversive Intervention for Behavior Problems: A Manual for Home and Community.* Baltimore: Paul H. Brookes.
Topper, K., W. Williams, K. Leo, R. Hamilton, and T. Fox. (1994). *A Positive Approach to Understanding and Addressing Challenging Behaviors: Supporting Educators and Families to Include Students with Emotional and Behavioral Difficulties in Regular Education.* Burlington, Vt.: The University Affiliated Program of Vermont.

Articles and Reports

Forest, M., and J. Pearpoint. (1990). "Supports for Addressing Severe Maladaptive Behaviors." In *Support Networks for Inclusive Schooling: Interdependent Integrated Education,* edited by W. Stainback and S. Stainback. Baltimore: Paul H. Brookes.
Goldstein, A.P. (1989). "Teaching Alternatives to Aggression." In *Schooling and Disability,* edited by D. Biklen, D.L. Ferguson, and A. Ford. Chicago: The National Society for the Study of Education.
Villa, R., J. Udis, and J. Thousand. (1994). "Creative Responses for Children Experiencing Behavioral and Emotional Challenges." In *Creativity and Collaborative Learning: A Practical Guide for Empowering Students and Teachers,* edited by J. Thousand, R. Villa, and A. Nevin. Baltimore: Paul H. Brookes.

Strategies for Promoting Belonging and Friendships

Books

Brendtro, L., M. Brokenleg, and S. Van Bockern. (1990). *Reclaiming Youth At Risk: Our Hope for the Future.* Bloomington, Ind.: National Educational Service.

Derman-Sparks, L., and the A.B.C. Task Force. (1989). *Anti-Bias Curriculum: Tools for Empowering Young Children.* Washington, D.C.: National Association for the Education of Young Children.

Schaffner, C.B., and B.E. Buswell. (1992). *Connecting Students: A Guide to Thoughtful Friendship Facilitation for Educators and Families.* Colorado Springs: PEAK Parent Center, Inc.

Schrumpf, F. (1994). "The Role of Students in Resolving Conflicts." In *Creativity and Collaborative Learning: A Practical Guide to Empowering Students and Teachers,* edited by J. Thousand, R. Villa, and A. Nevin. Baltimore: Paul H. Brookes.

Solomon, D., E. Schaps, M. Watson, and V. Battistich. (1992). "Creating Caring School and Classroom Communities for All Students." In *Restructuring for Caring and Effective Education: An Administrative Guide to Creating Heterogeneous Schools,* edited by R. Villa, J. Thousand, W. Stainback, and S. Stainback. Baltimore: Paul H. Brookes.

Vandercook, T. (1993). *Lessons for Inclusion.* Minneapolis: University of Minnesota, Institute on Community Integration, 109 Pattee Hall, 150 Pillsbury Drive SE, Minneapolis, MN 55455.

Articles and Reports

Biklen, D., C. Corrigan, and D. Quick. (1989). "Beyond Obligation: Students' Relations with Each Other in Integrated Classes." In *Beyond Separate Education: Quality Education for All,* edited by D.K. Lipsky and A. Gartner. Baltimore: Paul H. Brookes.

Falvey, M., M. Forest, J. Pearpoint, and R. Rosenberg. (1994). "Building Connections." In *Creativity and Collaborative Learning: A Practical Guide to Empowering Students and Teachers,* edited by J. Thousand, R. Villa, and A. Nevin. Baltimore: Paul H. Brookes.

Kuhmerker, L. (Fall 1989). "School Governance Structures That Foster Friendship in the Elementary School." *Equity and Choice,* pp. 34-41.

Kunc, N. (1992). "The Need to Belong." In *Restructuring for Caring and Effective Education: An Administrative Guide to Creating Heterogeneous Schools,* edited by R. Villa, J. Thousand, W. Stainback, and S. Stainback. Baltimore: Paul H. Brookes.

Sapon-Shevin, M. (1990). "Initial Steps for Developing a Caring School." In *Support Networks for Inclusive Schooling: Interdependent Integrated Education,* edited by W. Stainback and S. Stainback. Baltimore: Paul H. Brookes.

Sapon-Shevin, M. (Summer 1990). "Schools as Communities of Love and Caring." *Holistic Education Review* 11, 2: 22–24.

Schaffner, B., and B. Buswell. (1992). "What Is Friendship Facilitation?" In *Connecting Students: A Guide to Thoughtful Friendship Facilitation for Educators and Families.*,edited by B. Schaffner and B. Buswell. Colorado Springs: PEAK Parent Center, Inc.

Van Der Klift, E., and N. Kunc. (1994). "Beyond Benevolence: Friendship and the Politics of Help." In *Creativity and Collaborative Learning: A Practical Guide to Empowering Students and Teachers,* edited by J. Thousand, R. Villa, and A. Nevin. Baltimore: Paul H. Brookes.

Individual Advocacy and Systems Change Strategies

Buswell, B.E., and C.B. Schaffner. (1990). "Families Supporting Inclusive Schooling." In *Support Networks for Inclusive Schooling: Interdependent Integrated Education,* edited by W. Stainback and S. Stainback. Baltimore: Paul H. Brookes.

Nisbet, J.A., C. Jorgensen, and S. Powers. (1994). "Systems Change Directed at Inclusive Education." In *Creating Individual Supports for People with Developmental Disabilities: A Mandate for Change at Many Levels,* edited by V.T. Bradley, J.W. Ashbough, and B. Blaney. Baltimore: Paul H. Brookes.

Schaffner, C.B., and B.E. Buswell. (1989). *Breaking Ground: Ten Families Building Opportunities Through Integration.* Colorado Springs: PEAK Parent Center, Inc.

Differing Ability Information

Books

Nolan, C. (1987). *Under the Eye of the Clock: The Life Story of Christopher Nolan.* New York: St. Martin's Press.

Sapon-Shevin, M. (1994). *Playing Favorites: Gifted Education and the Disruption of Community.* Albany, N.Y.: State University of New York Press.

Williams, D. (1992). *Nobody, Nowhere: The Extraordinary Autobiography of an Autistic.* New York: Times Books.

Reports and Articles

Copeland, E., and V. Love. (1992). *Attention Without Tension: A Teacher's Handbook on Attention Disorders.* Atlanta, Ga.: 3 C's of Childhood Incorporated.

Esposito, B.G., and M.A. Koorland. (1989). "Play Behavior of Hearing-Impaired Children: Integrated and Segregated Settings." *Exceptional Children* 55, 5: 412-419.

Fox, C. (1989). "Peer Acceptance of Learning Disabled Children in the Regular Classroom." *Exceptional Children* 56, 1: 50-59.

Heron, L. (Spring 1994). "Success for Students with Learning Disabilities in Inclusive Classrooms: More than Cosmetic Changes Are Needed." *Equity and Excellence* 1, 1: 15-17. (Available from Institute on Disability, Heidelberg-Harris Building, University of New Hampshire, Durham, NH 03824.)

Leone, P., M. McLaughlin, and M. Meisel. (1992). "School Reform and Adolescents with Behavior Disorders." *Focus on Exceptional Children* 25, 1: 1-15.

McLeskey, J., and D. Pacchianp. (1994). "Mainstreaming Students with Learning Disabilities: Are We Making Progress?" *Exceptional Children* 60, 6: 508-517.

Videocassettes

AGH Associates, Inc. (1993). *Plain Talk: Teacher to Teacher.* Hampton, N.H.: Ann G. Haggart Associates, Inc., Box 130, Hampton, NH 03843. Phone: (603) 926-1316. 27 minutes.

Association for Supervision and Curriculum Development. (1995). *Inclusion: Educating All Students, Strategies for Success, and Profiles of Successful Students.* Alexandria, Va.: ASCD. 85 minutes (3-tape set; 25-35 minutes each).

British Columbia Association for Community Living. (1990). *Hello, My Friends.* Vancouver, British Columbia: Jon Stoddart Productions Inc. 17 minutes. (Order through: Expectations Unlimited, Inc., P.O. Box 655, Niwot, CO 80544.)

Burrello, L., J. Burrello, and J. Winniger, producers. (1993). *The Inclusion Series— The Two Faces of Inclusion: The Concept and the Practice.* Bloomington: Indiana University. 56 minutes.

Buzzell, J.B., and R. Piazza, producers. (1994). *Case Studies for Teaching Special Needs and At-Risk Students.* Albany, N.Y.: Delmar Publishers.

District 742 Media Services Productions. (N.d.) *A Recipe for Life.* St. Cloud, Minn.: District 742 Community Schools, DMS Studios, St. Cloud, MN 56301. Phone: (612) 252-8770. Approximately 5 minutes.

Godwin, T., and G. Wurzburg, producers. (1988). *Regular Lives.* Washington, D.C.: State of the Art Productions.

Graff, W., G. Lambert, R. Villa, and J. Thousand, producers. (1992). *Student Collaboration: An Essential for Curriculum Delivery in the 21st Century.* 26 minutes.(Available from George Cross, Winooski School District, 60 Normand St., Winooski, VT 05404.)

Graff, W., G. Lambert, R. Villa, and J. Thousand, producers. (1992). *Peer Power: Collaborating to Meet the Needs of a Diverse Student Population.* 29 minutes. (Available from George Cross, Winooski School District, 60 Normand St., Winooski, VT 05404.)

Linton Productions. (1994). *Inclusion.* Salt Lake City: The Video Journal of Education, 5499 West 3560 South, Salt Lake City, UT 84115-4225. 66 minutes (2-video set; 33 minutes each).

Home Box Office, producer. (1993). *Educating Peter.* New York: Ambrose Video Publishing, 1290 Avenue of the Americas, Suite 2245, New York, NY 10104. 30 minutes.

Institute on Disability. (1992). *Dream Catchers.* Concord, N.H.: University of New Hampshire, Institute on Disability, The Concord Center, Box 14, 10 Ferry St., Concord, NH 03301. 16 minutes.

The People First Association of Lethbridge. (1990). *Kids Belong Together.* Niwot, Colo.: Expectations Unlimited, P.O. Box 655, Niwot, CO 80544. 30 minutes.

Tomerlin, J., producer. (1994). *Inclusion: Friends for Life.* Media Inc., Box 496, Media, PA 19063.

World Interdependence Fund. (1994). *Discover Interdependence.* Sacramento, Calif.: World Interdependence Fund.

About the Authors

Richard A. Villa, Co-editor of *Creating an Inclusive School*, is President of the Bayridge Educational Consortium, 6 Bayridge Estates, Colchester, VT 05446. Voice/Fax: 802-878-8957. E-mail: 74642.711@compuserve.com

Jacqueline S. Thousand, Co-editor of *Creating an Inclusive School*, is Research Associate Professor at the College of Education and Social Services and University Affiliated Facility, 449C Waterman Building, University of Vermont, Burlington, VT 05405. Voice: 802-656-1146; Fax: 802-656-1357. E-mail: jthousan@moose.uvm.edu

Barbara E. Buswell, Co-director, PEAK Parent Center, Inc.; Director, TAPP Focus Center on Inclusion. Address: PEAK Parent Center, Inc., 6055 Lehman Drive, Colorado Springs, CO 80918. Voice: 719-531-9400.

James W. Chapple, Instructional Resources Coordinator, Northern Ohio Special Education Regional Resource Center, 218 North Pleasant Street, Oberlin, OH 44074. Voice: 216-775-2786; Fax: 216-775-3713. E-mail: jchapp@leeca8.leeca.ohio.gov

Lia Cravedi-Cheng, Lecturer, University of Vermont, College of Education and Social Services, Waterman Building, Burlington, VT 05405. Voice: 802-656-1352; Fax: 802-656-1357.

Mary A. Falvey, Professor, Division of Special Education, California State University, 5151 State University Drive, Los Angeles, CA 90032. Voice: 213-343-4416; Fax: 213-343-5605. E-mail: mfalvey@calstatela.edu

Christine C. Givner, Associate Professor, Division of Special Education, California State University-Los Angeles, 5151 State University Drive, Los Angeles, CA 90032. Voice: 213-343-4406; Fax: 213-343-5605. E-mail: cgivner@calstatela.edu

Nancy Keller, Middle Grades Science Teacher, Winooski School District, 80 Normand Street, Winooski, VT 05404. Voice: 802-655-3530. E-mail: keller@smcvax.smcvt.edu

Christina Kimm, Associate Professor, Division of Special Education, California State University-Los Angeles, 5151 State University Drive, Los Angeles, CA 90032. Voice: 213-343-4416; Fax: 213-343-5605. E-mail: ckimm@calstatela.edu

Norman Kunc, Educational Consultant and Co-director, Axis Consultation & Training Limited, 4623 Elizabeth Street, Port Alberni, British Columbia, Canada V9Y6L8. Voice: 604-723-6644; Fax: 604-723-6688.

Ann I. Nevin, Professor, College of Education, Arizona University West, Phoenix, AZ 85069-7100. Voice: 602-543-6329; Fax: 602-543-6350. E-mail: ICAX@asuvm.inre.asu.edu

C. Beth Schaffner, Coordinator of Inclusive Schooling, PEAK Parent Center, Inc.; Technical Assistance Facilitator, TAPP Focus Center on Inclusion. Address: PEAK Parent Center, Inc., 6055 Lehman Drive, Colorado Springs, CO 80918. Voice: 719-531-9400.

Susan Stainback, Professor of Education, Department of Special Education, College of Education, University of Northern Iowa, Cedar Falls, IA 50613. Voice: 319-273-6064.

William Stainback, Professor of Education, Department of Special Education, College of Education, University of Northern Iowa, Cedar Falls, IA 50613. Voice: 319-273-6064.

Jeff Tate, Chair, Austin, Texas, Chapter of Schools Are for Everyone (SAFE), The ARC of Texas, Project Jobs, 11600 W. 38th St., Suite 200, P.O. Box 5368, Austin, TX 78763.

Jonathan Udis, Educational Consultant, P.O. Box 3368, RD#3, Montpelier, VT 05602. Phone/Fax: 802-229-4616.

Alice Udvari-Solner, Assistant Professor, Department of Curriculum and Instruction and Department of Rehabilitation Psychology and Special Education, University of Wisconsin-Madison, 255 North Mill Street, Room 2448, Madison, WI 53706. Voice: 608-263-4645; Fax: 608-263-9992. E-mail: alice@mail.soe.madison.wisc.edu

Emma Van der Klift, Educational Consultant and Co-director, Axis Consultation & Training Limited, 4623 Elizabeth Street, Port Alberni, British Columbia, Canada V9Y6L8. Voice: 604-723-6644; Fax: 604-723-6688.

Joe Vargo, parent consultant/advocate, 111 Schuler Street, Syracuse, NY 13203. Voice: 315-422-7796. Fax: 315-422-4139.

Rosalind Vargo, parent consultant/advocate, 111 Schuler Street, Syracuse, NY 13203. Voice: 315-422-7796. Fax: 315-422-4139.

Selected ASCD Resources Related to Creating an Inclusive School

ASCD Select Resource Packets

Resource packets of articles, abstracts, and other documents on various topics, drawn from:

- *Educational Leadership*
- ASCD *Update* and *Curriculum Update*
- *Curriculum/Technology Quarterly*
- *Journal of Curriculum and Supervision*
- other sources available in the public domain

Each packet includes two disks (DOS only):

- *ASCD Resources Diskette* (brief descriptions of *all* ASCD products and services)
- *Educational Leadership Abstracts* from September 1989 through May 1994.

Each packet also includes a discount coupon for a savings of 10 percent on any one ASCD product. Call ASCD at (703) 549-9110, ext. 518 or 507, for information about other topics. Price for each packet: $34.95. The following Resource Packets are particularly relevant to this book:

Assessment/Portfolio Assessment, Stock # Select 02
Grouping/Nongraded Instruction, Stock # Select 07
Inclusion, Stock # Select 23
Restructuring/Reform, Stock # Select 13
Technology, Stock # Select 18

ASCD Books

Cooperative Learning in the Classroom, by David W. Johnson, Roger T. Johnson, and Edythe J. Holubec, 1994. 110 pages. Stock # 1-94224. $13.95

A Different Kind of Classroom: Teaching with Dimensions of Learning, by Robert Marzano, 1992. 191 pp. Stock # 611-92107. $15.95. Part of ASCD and Midcontinent Regional Educational Laboratory's Dimension of Learning program. *Trainer's Manual*, *Teacher's Manual*, and accompanying video also available. Call ASCD at 1-800-933-2723 for information.

How to Differentiate Instruction in Mixed-Ability Classrooms, by Carol Ann Tomlinson, 1995. 80 pp. Stock # 195184. $6.95

In Search of Understanding: The Case for Constructivist Classrooms, by Jacqueline Grennon Brooks and Martin G. Brooks, 1993. 136 pp. Stock # 611-93148. $13.95.

Multiple Intelligences in the Classroom, by Thomas Armstrong, 1994. 186 pp. Stock # 1-94055. $14.95.

ASCD Video-Based Staff Development Programs

Cooperative Learning. Program consultants: Robert Slavin, Roger Johnson, David Johnson, and Britt Vasquez. 5-tape set and *Facilitator's Manual*: Stock # 614-201. Purchase of entire set: $980 (ASCD members).

Inclusion. Including special education students in the general education environment, in cooperation with the Council for Exceptional Children. 3-tape set and *Facilitator's Guide*; Stock # 4-95044. Purchase of entire set: $680 (ASCD members).

What's New in School—A Parent's Guide. Four tapes, with presentation guides and parent handouts, on cooperative learning, curriculum integration, and performance assessment. Stock # 4-94178. Purchase of entire set: $135 (ASCD members).

ASCD Audiotapes

Guiding Performance-Based Teaching and Learning. A set of three 40- to 60-minute audiotapes: (1) "Major Beliefs Guiding Performance-Based Education," (2) "Fundamental Principles of Performance-Based Tasks and Rubrics," and (3) "Structural Changes Needed to Support Performance-Based Teaching and Learning," by Heidi Hayes Jacobs, Robert Marzano, Debra Pickering, and Grant Wiggins. Stock # 2-95039. $29.00.

The Mainstreamed School: Interventions to Meet Student Needs. ASCD Professional Development Institute (on 6 audiotapes) with *Presenter's Notebook*. Presenter: Dick Sagor. Stock # 295013. $89.00.

Teaching Thinking to Multiple Intelligences and Diverse Student Populations. Presenter: Richard Strong. Stock # 2-94022. $9.95.

ASCD Networks

Adaptive Strategies for Inclusion. Facilitator: *Jane Oates,* Temple University, 989 Ritter Annex, 13th & Cecil B. Moore Ave., Philadelphia, PA 19122. Phone: (215) 204-4529, FAX: (215) 204-5130.

African-American Critical Issues. Facilitator: *Peyton Williams,* Associate Deputy State Supt. Ext. Affairs, Department of Education, Office of Instructional Programs, 1966 Twin Towers East, Atlanta, GA 30334-5040. Phone: (404) 657-7410, FAX: (404) 657-6978.

Authentic Assessment. Facilitators: *Kathleen Busick,* Pacific Region Education Lab, 828 Fort Street Mall, Mall 500, Honolulu, HI 96813. Phone: (808) 533-6000 ext. 131, FAX: (808) 533-7599; *Judith Dorsch Backes,* Carroll County Public Schools, 55 North Court Street, Westminster, MD 21157. Phone: (410) 848-8280, FAX: (410) 876-9224.

Multi-Age Classroom. Facilitators: *Jane Raphael*, Mentor Teacher, Los Angeles Unified SD, Wonderland Ave. Elem. School, 8510 Wonderland Avenue, Los Angeles, CA 90046. Phone: (213) 654-4401, FAX: (213) 656-3228; *Meredith Adams*, Monte Vista Street School, Los Angeles USD, 5423 Monte Vista Street, Los Angeles, CA 90042. Phone: (213) 344-9759.

Teaching for Multiple Intelligences. Facilitator: *David G. Lazear*, New Dimensions of Learning, 729 West Waveland, Suite G, Chicago, IL 60613. Phone: (312) 525-6650.

For information on these and other networks, contact the ASCD Networks Program, ext. 503 or 504.

ASCD

Association for Supervision and Curriculum Development
1250 North Pitt Street
Alexandria, VA 22314

Phone: 1-800-933-2723
Fax: (703) 549-3891
Internet: info@ascd.org
World Wide Web Home Page: http://www.ascd.org